Get Updates and More on Nolo.com

Go to this book's companion page at:

www.nolo.com/back-of-book/ESPN.html

When there's an important change to the law affecting this book, we'll post updates. You'll also find articles and other related materials.

More Resources from Nolo.com

Legal Forms, Books, & Software

Hundreds of do-it-yourself products—all written in plain English, approved, and updated by our in-house legal editors.

Legal Articles

Get informed with thousands of free articles on everyday legal topics. Our articles are accurate, up to date, and reader friendly.

Find a Lawyer

Want to talk to a lawyer? Use Nolo to find a lawyer who can help you with your case.

NOLO
LAW for ALL

10th Edition

Estate Planning Basics

Attorney Denis Clifford

TENTH EDITION	FEBRUARY 2020
Editor	BETSY SIMMONS HANNIBAL
Book and Cover Design	SUSAN PUTNEY
Production	SUSAN PUTNEY
Proofreader	ROBERT WELLS
Index	VICTORIA BAKER
Printing	BANG PRINTING

ISSN: 2167-5481 (print)
ISSN: 2328-4757 (online)

ISBN: 978-1-4133-2669-7 (pbk)
ISBN: 978-1-4133-2670-3 (ebook)

This book covers only United States law, unless it specifically states otherwise.

Please note

We believe accurate, plain-English legal information should help you solve many of your own legal problems. But this text is not a substitute for personalized advice from a knowledgeable lawyer. If you want the help of a trained professional—and we'll always point out situations in which we think that's a good idea—consult an attorney licensed to practice in your state.

Dedication

To my Sisters and Brothers: Catherine, Justin, Douglas, Gregory, Steve, and Joanne.

Acknowledgments

My thanks and gratitude to:

Betsy Simmons Hannibal, once again, for being a superb editor and easy to work with;

My other editors at Nolo: Jake Warner, Steve Elias, Mary Randolph, and Shae Irving for all their help over many years;

Stan Jacobsen, Nolo officemate and kindred spirit;

Toni Ihara for connecting me with Nolo, and her friendship for decades;

And, as ever, to Naomi.

About the Author

Denis Clifford practices estate planning law in Berkeley, California. He is the author of several Nolo books, including *Plan Your Estate* and *Make Your Own Living Trust*. A graduate of Columbia Law School, where he was an editor of the *Columbia Law Review*, he has practiced law in various ways, and is convinced that people can do much of the legal work they need themselves.

Table of Contents

Appendix

Index

Your Estate Planning Legal Companion

If you're like a lot of people, you have a nagging feeling that you need to work on your estate plan—but you haven't gotten around to it because it sounds hard or expensive or just unpleasant. Perhaps you don't even know where to start. We're here to help. In *Estate Planning Basics*, attorney and estate planning expert Denis Clifford gives you a broad overview of the nuts and bolts of estate planning and clearly explains what you'll need to consider while planning your estate.

What is estate planning, anyway? It may sound mysterious, but it doesn't have to be. At its core, estate planning is deciding who will get your property after you die and choosing how that property will be transferred at your death. Estate planning can also mean making some important personal decisions, such as who will provide care for your young children if you cannot and who should make medical and financial decisions for you if you become unable to handle things yourself.

It may not be easy to think about these deeply personal issues, but creating a plan that puts your affairs in order does not need to be complicated or difficult. And the sooner you get your plan in place, the sooner you can reap the real reward of estate planning: the feeling of confidence and security that comes with knowing that the people you love will be taken care of after you're gone.

To help you get going with your estate plan, this book explains:
- how wills work and why you need one
- the benefits of using a living trust
- how you can to provide care and protection for your children
- what probate is and why you want to avoid it
- the ins and outs of the main retirement savings plans
- preparing for incapacity

- estate taxes—and why it's highly unlikely that you need to worry about them
- how to make your own estate plan, and
- when you need to see a lawyer.

When you're ready to actually make your plan, you'll probably be able to do much of your estate planning yourself, if you want to. Many estate planning tools, including wills, simple living trusts, health care directives, and powers of attorney usually do not need a lawyer's expensive touch. Most of these tools are simple, relatively inexpensive, and available to regular people. Of course, there can certainly be situations when an attorney's help is desirable. But the reality is that you'll be able to get a good start on, and perhaps finish, your estate plan without ever needing to hire a lawyer.

Congratulations on starting your estate planning—it's a wonderful thing to do for yourself and your family. We know from long experience that putting a sound estate plan into place can bring peace and satisfaction to those who take the time to do it.

Get Updates and More Online

When there are important changes to the information in this book, we'll post updates online, on a page dedicated to this book:

www.nolo.com/back-of-book/ESPN.html

A First Look at Estate Planning

Who needs to bother with estate planning? Here's the short answer:
- anyone who owns property that matters to them
- anyone with a minor child (under 18), and
- anyone concerned with possible incapacity.

Estate planning isn't only for the rich, nor are there minimum property requirements, such as owning a home. Anything you care about—from artworks to gold earrings to items with little or no market value such as the old family rocking chair or loved photographs—is significant enough to warrant at least basic estate planning.

The key is to ask yourself whether you own any property that you want to go to a specific person or organization when you die. If the answer is yes, you need to create a plan to make sure your desires will be carried out.

> **EXAMPLE:** Tracy told me she had no reason to worry about estate planning; she was a carpenter. I asked her if she was sure she owned nothing she cared about. She answered "No, nothing—well, I guess my tools." When I pressed her a bit, she estimated they were worth, in total, over $35,000. I told her that if she did no planning before she died, her tools would be divided, according to state law, among members of her family. She exclaimed that wasn't what she wanted at all. Everyone knew she wanted her tools to go to her partner, Alex. I explained that she could guarantee her goal by preparing a very simple will. Later, having prepared a will, she told me, "You know, that's been nagging at me for years." I answered that she was definitely not alone.

If you have a minor child, or children, you automatically have estate planning concerns. Who will raise your child if you can't? More precisely, if you and the child's other parent, if there is one involved, die before your child is a legal adult (over 18), who will be the adult responsible for caring for the child? Legally, there are two different adult roles involved. The first is raising and nurturing the child—having legal custody, and making day-to-day personal decisions on the child's behalf. The second adult role is managing any property owned by, or left for the use of, the child. By law, minors cannot control any significant amount of property they own. Commonly, parents name one adult to serve in both capacities.

> **EXAMPLE:** Felicity and Joe have two young children, ages one and three. They own an inexpensive car, personal and household belongings, and two life insurance policies for $100,000, one on each spouse's life. If one parent dies, the other one will, of course, carry on. But like many parents, the couple worries about what will happen if they die together. They discuss who should raise their children and manage the insurance money if they both die. They are pleased and relieved to agree that their wisest choice is Joe's sister Susan, who loves their kids and is securely married with one child of her own. Felicity and Joe discuss the matter with Susan, who agrees to serve as guardian if the need arises.
>
> Joe and Felicity also are aware that present stability is no guarantee of lifetime security. If Susan's life drastically changes for the worse, Joe and Felicity will then make new plans for the care of their children.

Estate planning is also a good idea for anyone who has any concern about future incapacity. For most people, this concern centers around what would happen if you become incapacitated and can no longer manage your finances or make your own health care decisions. The wise way to handle these possibilities is to create binding legal documents that set out your wishes and appoint a person of your choice to make decisions for you if you can't. (See Chapter 4.)

RESOURCE
Learn about your state's intestate succession laws. If you die without a will, your state's "intestate succession" laws will determine how your property will be distributed. You learn about your state's intestate succession laws on Nolo.com at www.nolo.com/legal-encyclopedia/intestate-succession.

I'm Not Ready

I've thought of putting that phrase on my tombstone, though I decided instead to use what I cried out as a child whenever my parents asked me to do a chore: "Right now?" But, all kidding aside, "I'm not ready" is how many people feel about estate planning. There are some understandable reasons for this procrastination: a busy life, a mistrust of lawyers, a sense that estate planning is boring. I suspect, though, that there's often something more primitive at work: at least a touch of superstition, a fear that thinking about death might somehow hasten its occurrence.

If you procrastinate until death, that could prove costly to your inheritors, and may well mean that your property will not be distributed as you wish. If you die without a will or other valid transfer device, your property will be divided between family members according to a formula established by state law. A judge will appoint someone to supervise the distribution of your property. Your estate must pay this person's fee, which can become quite hefty.

Similarly, if you have minor children and the other parent is not available or suitable for custody, you won't want to take the chance that you'll have no input regarding who will raise the children if you can't. Estate planning is also a good idea for anyone who has any concern about future incapacity. For most people, this concern centers around what would happen if you become incapacitated and can no longer manage your finances or make your own health care decisions. The wise way to handle these possibilities is to create binding legal documents that set out your wishes and appoint a person of your choice to make decisions for you if you can't. (See Chapter 4.)

In sum, ready or not, it's wise to get your estate planning done soon.

Basic estate planning has just a few branches. I'll sketch them out here; these subjects are then covered in more depth in subsequent chapters.

Evaluating Your Personal Situation

The first step in creating a sound estate plan is to look realistically at your unique personal situation. You could start with a few questions: Are you married, partnered, or single? Do you have kids? Are you in a second or subsequent marriage or relationship? If so, do you have a blended family? Stepchildren? Do you have any children from prior relationships? Do you have grandchildren? Brothers and sisters? Other close family members? Who else do you care about and want to leave property to, beyond your close relatives? Are there any causes, charities, or other institutions to which you want to leave property?

For some, perhaps many people, these are not hard questions to answer; they don't raise difficulties or complexities. Others don't have it so easy. Thinking about family members can bring up worries about fights over property, or people you don't care for, or a number of awkward or painful situations that have fueled novels and movies for as long as these arts have existed.

Some people's situations have built-in complications. For example, one or both people in a second or subsequent marriage may have children from earlier relationships. Many couples have "his, hers, and our" kids. Some have "his, her, and our" property as well. Deciding how to divide property between the children may not be easy. Plus there are often other concerns. For instance, after a spouse dies, suppose the surviving spouse needs the deceased spouse's property to maintain his or her lifestyle. Perhaps the couple shared ownership of a house or condominium. Can the surviving spouse continue to live there, while preserving the deceased spouse's share for children of prior marriages? Estate planning for second or subsequent marriages is discussed in Chapter 2; the use of trusts to control property from such marriages is covered in Chapter 11.

Single people can have different, but equally important concerns. Single parents will naturally be concerned about who will raise their minor children if they cannot. (See Chapter 3.) Also, a single person may not be sure whom to name as executor of his or her estate. (See Chapter 5.)

A therapy guide this book is not, so I won't launch into extended psychological discussions here about handling personal or family problems. What's important is that you reflect on and address any problems you want or need to deal with when you leave your property.

One subject to ponder is whether there's anyone you want to discuss your plans with. If you're married or partnered, you'll almost certainly have an in-depth discussion with your mate. Beyond that, you have to decide what is wise. As you plan, do you want to discuss your planning with family members or other major beneficiaries? Sometimes, candid discussion can help you make the best decisions.

Your Property

At the heart of your estate plan will be decisions about who will inherit your property. But before you can make those decisions, you must know what you own.

Knowing What You Own

Many people, especially those doing basic estate planning, face no problem knowing what property they own. Often the major asset is a house; then there's a car, some savings, perhaps stocks or other investments, and personal or household possessions, like jewelry or art. There may be other assets, such as any funds remaining in retirement accounts like an IRA or a 401(k) plan, where beneficiaries are named as part of the asset. (Using retirement plans as estate planning devices is discussed in Chapter 8.)

You don't necessarily have to prepare an itemized list of your property to do your estate planning. Indeed, most people don't need to bother with it, especially if you plan to leave all or most of your property to one or more people. However, some people find it helpful. Inventorying your property can be particularly desirable if:

- You plan to leave many items of property to many different beneficiaries—for example, a large collection of jazz records to be distributed among dozens of fellow aficionados.
- You are not sure what you actually own, perhaps because of shared business ownership, or because you're not certain about your state's rules governing marital property for estate planning purposes. (See "A Spouse's Right to Inherit Property," below.)
- You want to pin down what you own so you can estimate your net worth to see if your estate is likely to owe federal estate tax. But even here, a rough estimate of total value is all you need, and you probably won't have to itemize meticulously to make that estimate.

If you decide you do need an itemized list of your property, many of Nolo's hands-on estate planning resources provide thorough checklists of all significant types of property so you won't overlook, say, your gas and oil royalties or valuable patents.

TIP

Don't forget your digital assets. When thinking about what should happen to your property when you die, consider what will happen to the things you keep online—blogs, email accounts, photos, social networking identities, and so on. You won't be able to use your will or trust to leave most of these things to others, but you can leave detailed instructions for your executor describing what you'd like done with them. It's also a good idea to securely leave a list of your user names and passwords, so that your executor won't have any trouble accessing your accounts. You can learn more about planning for your digital assets at www.nolo.com/legal-encyclopedia/digital-assets.

A Spouse's Right to Inherit Property

In the great majority of states, called "common law" states, your spouse has a legal right to inherit part of your property. In these states, laws protect a surviving spouse from being completely disinherited by the other spouse. If a spouse isn't left at least the amount required by state statute—usually one-half of the deceased spouse's property—the surviving spouse can claim that amount, no matter what the deceased spouse's estate plan provided. In almost all common law states, a spouse can waive his or her statutory inheritance rights. This can be done in a prenuptial agreement, or at any later time.

Common Law and Community Property States	
Common law states are all states that aren't community property states.	**Community property** states are Arizona, California*, Idaho, Louisiana, Nevada, New Mexico, Texas, Washington*, and Wisconsin.

Alaska, South Dakota, and Tennessee allow a married couple to create a written agreement or trust defining some or all of their property as community property.

* Registered domestic partners are also covered by community property laws.

In contrast, "community property" states have no inheritance requirements for spouses. Instead, spouses are protected by the rule that each spouse owns one-half of all property acquired by either spouse during marriage. There are, of course, some exceptions. For example, property owned by one spouse before marriage and kept separate during the marriage remains the separate property of that spouse, as does property inherited by or gifted to one spouse.

SEE AN EXPERT

Planning to leave your spouse less than half. If you live in a common law state, and you want to leave your spouse less than one-half of your property, see a lawyer for advice.

Choosing Your Beneficiaries

Your beneficiaries (W.C. Fields called them "bean-fisheries") are the people and organizations to which you leave your property. Distribution plans can range from the simple, such as leaving everything to your spouse, to far more complex arrangements, such as using trusts to leave property to many family members over generations while also leaving property to friends and organizations at your death.

As I've said, you decide who gets your property. I've found that most people who start estate planning know who their beneficiaries will be. You're unlikely to need a lawyer's help here; the most a good one could do is help you clarify your own desires if you feel confused or conflicted, or perhaps point out some difficulties that might arise if you're considering a complex beneficiary plan. But most people face no serious problem choosing beneficiaries. The key components of a simple beneficiary situation are that your choices are clear, and that you leave your property outright, with no strings or controls attached. (One exception can be property left to minors or young adults. See "Choosing How Your Children's Property Should Be Managed," in Chapter 3.)

> **EXAMPLE 1:** Francine and Phillip, a married couple, want to leave everything to each other. When the second spouse dies, all the property will be divided equally among their three children.

> **EXAMPLE 2:** Lily has a son, age nine, and a modest estate. She wants to leave most of her property to her son (in a trust until he's 30), and the remainder to her friends Kelly and Gretchen.

EXAMPLE 3: Angela has a substantial estate, and two children, ages 45 and 36. She wants to leave the bulk of her property equally to them, plus gifts of specific heirlooms to her sister and niece, and some cash to The Nature Society.

As I've said, couples in second, or subsequent, marriages may face more difficult beneficiary decisions. If one or both spouses have children from a prior marriage, conflicting desires can arise. Spouses may feel torn between leaving property to children from a prior marriage and aiding the current spouse, along with any children from the new marriage.

EXAMPLE: Russell and Katy marry in their 50s, a second marriage for both of them. Russell has two children, ages 25 and 28. Katy has a daughter, who just turned 30. Russell's net worth is about $370,000; Katy's is about $560,000. They purchase a house together. Each contributes $150,000 for the down payment. Katy will pay roughly two-thirds of the mortgage payments and house expenses, because she earns considerably more than Russell.

Both spouses feel strongly that when one spouse dies, the other should be able to continue to live in the house. But they also want their individual shares of the house to go to their own children after they both die. Neither wants to create the possibility that the child or children of the spouse who lives the longest could somehow end up owning the entire house. The couple must agree on how the house will be divided when both die, including how Katy's extra contribution for payments and expenses will be apportioned. Also, they must devise a legal mechanism to accomplish their goals.

The usual legal device for handling this kind of second-marriage issue is a particular type of trust; I call it a "marital property control trust." I discuss this type of trust in Chapter 11.

Providing for Young Children

Parents raising young children are usually quite clear that their major estate planning concern is providing for the minors if the parents suddenly die. (A minor is any child under age 18.) "Providing" means deciding both who will raise the child and who will manage any money or property that the child legally owns. It may also include making plans to have sufficient property to leave the child, such as buying term life insurance. These concerns are discussed in depth in Chapter 3, but because they are so central to many people, I'll focus on a few important points here.

Custody of Your Children

If the other parent is involved and survives you, that parent will normally take custody of the children. On the other hand, if there is no other parent involved, or to prepare for the possibility of the death of both you and the other parent, you can use your will to nominate a "personal guardian" who will care for your children. Your nomination is not binding on a court, however, because children are not property and cannot be willed to someone. But if custody is not contested, which is true for the great majority of cases where a child's parent or parents die, the judge will routinely confirm the expressed desires of the deceased parent.

> EXAMPLE: Myron and Kim are divorced but manage to cooperate without viciousness in raising their young son Lawrence. Each understands that if one dies before Lawrence turns 18, the other parent will have custody. Myron dies and Kim now has sole custody. In her will, she nominates her sister Polly to serve as Lawrence's guardian if she dies.

It's very difficult to prevent a parent who has been involved in raising a child from gaining legal custody if the custodial parent dies. But if the other parent has not been involved in raising the child, or you believe that parent is not fit to have custody, there are steps you can take to try to prevent that parent from gaining custody. (See "Naming Someone to Care for Young Children," in Chapter 3.)

> EXAMPLE: Jeannette is a single mother of five-year-old Sam. Sam's biological father has never had anything to do with Sam, neither parenting nor contributing money for child support. If she cannot raise her son, Jeannette wants her brother and his wife, not Sam's biological father, to raise him. While Jeannette cannot guarantee this result, she can prepare a detailed written statement that explains why her brother would be the proper guardian. This statement could be very persuasive to a judge who must decide who would be the best person to raise Sam.

Your Children's Property

Legally, minors cannot own any significant amount of property outright, more than $2,500 to $5,000 depending on the state. So you need to nominate an adult to supervise and manage any property owned by your child, including property you leave to the child, other inheritances, or the child's own earnings. There are several different legal devices you can use to leave property to your young children. These are discussed in Chapter 3.

Planning for Incapacity

When you begin making plans to leave your property, there's one other vital issue to address: It's crucial that you make arrangements for the handling of your medical and financial affairs if you ever become incapacitated and can't take care of them yourself. Wrenching family conflicts can arise if you haven't clearly specified your wishes. Creating binding legal documents that express your desires is discussed in Chapter 4.

Protecting Assets in Case of Catastrophic Illness
Many people are concerned that if they become seriously ill, all their assets will be consumed to pay for health care costs. To address this reasonable concern, some people hope that there is a simple clause or trust they can use to shield their assets. Unfortunately, no such device exists. The best you can do is: (1) Seek advice from an attorney who is knowledgeable about the type of (complex and expensive) trusts that could protect your assets, such as a "Medicaid trust" or a "domestic asset protection trust." (2) If you're married or coupled, learn how to protect the assets of the spouse or partner who isn't ill. This is covered in depth in *Long-Term Care: How to Plan & Pay for It*, by Joseph L. Matthews (Nolo).

Transferring Your Property After You Die

To arrange for the transfer of your property to your beneficiaries after you die, you must use one or some combination of various legal devices. The two most popular are wills and living trusts. Deciding which transfer devices are best for you is the main technical aspect of basic estate planning, and it's where law and legal documents come into play.

At this point, some estate planning books start insisting that you hire lawyers, warning of the disasters that will befall those who dare to try to handle their own affairs without paying thousands of dollars for professional help. As I've already stressed, this is nonsense. Most readers will learn that by applying their own common sense, they can safely select which device or combination of devices is best for them, without hiring a lawyer.

Wills

A will, the simplest estate planning device to prepare, is a document that leaves some or all of your property to beneficiaries you choose. You can also use a will to name an adult guardian for your young children. Wills are discussed in detail in Chapter 5.

The principal drawback of a will is that it must normally go through probate, a complicated and expensive court proceeding. Probate rarely provides any real benefit to your beneficiaries, or, indeed, to anyone, except the lawyers involved. (See "Probate," in Chapter 5.)

Living Trusts

A living trust is a legal document similar to a will in function, except that no probate or other court proceedings are required to turn property over to beneficiaries. Because of this, living trusts are a popular probate-avoidance device. A living trust can only distribute property that is legally owned by the trust. So, you must legally transfer property to your trust when or after you create it. (See Chapter 6.)

Other Ways to Transfer Property

There are a number of other ways to transfer property—and avoid probate—that can be useful in certain situations. These methods include:

- pay-on-death accounts for bank deposits or securities (stocks and bonds)
- transfer-on-death real estate deeds
- transfer-on-death vehicle registration
- joint tenancy, a form of ownership where the surviving owner(s) automatically receive the interest of a deceased owner without probate, and

- tenancy by the entirety, a special version of joint tenancy specifically limited to married people.

These and other easy ways to avoid probate are discussed at greater length in Chapter 7.

Estate Taxes

Don't worry about estate taxes until you find out whether or not your estate will owe them. Almost all will not. For deaths in 2020, an estate must be worth over $11.58 million (net) before it's liable for federal estate taxes. This amount will rise with inflation. (For more, see "Federal Estate Tax Exemptions," in Chapter 9.)

Making Changes

You are not locked into anything when you prepare your estate plan, including your basic documents, such as your will or living trust. With a couple of exceptions, you can change, amend, or revoke your documents any time you want to, for any reason—or for no reason. (Joint tenancy is a special case; see "Joint Tenancy," in Chapter 7. Also, some types of estate tax-saving trusts must be irrevocable while you live. See "Tax-Saving Irrevocable Trusts," in Chapter 10.)

The only limitation is that you must be "competent" when you make a change. Legally, "competence" means having the mental capacity to make and understand decisions regarding your property. You have to be pretty far gone before you aren't legally competent to change your documents. For instance, forgetfulness, including not always remembering who people are, does not by itself establish mental incompetence.

Some Thoughts About Death

Though this book concentrates on practical matters, I want to acknowledge the deepest reality involved—death itself.

We all experience the loss of family and friends; it's the human condition. Years now after his death, I continue to feel recurrent grief and loss at the tragic, unfathomable (to me) death of my friend (and fellow Nolo author) Hayden Curry.

Coping with the death of a loved one is intensely personal. Some people are fortunate to have religious beliefs, traditions, rituals, and ceremonies to help. Others find sources of solace and inspiration in nature, or from sacred works, or poetry. This is not a book of philosophy or religion, so I merely note that each person must seek to find his or her own acceptance—if not understanding—of death.

However you are able to deal with the fact of death, it's no denigration of that reality to arrange for your desired handling of your affairs. After all, the effects of sensible estate planning benefit the living. Estate planning is a gift to those you love.

The people I've been close to who have died all prepared thorough estate plans. I saw and understood how important it was for them to know that they hadn't left a mess for their friends and family to clean up, and that they had directed that their property go where they thought it would be most beneficial.

More Estate Planning Resources From Nolo

At Nolo we are, of course, in favor of do-it-yourself law and avoiding lawyers whenever that's feasible. Below is a list of Nolo products that are useful for different aspects of estate planning and related matters.

- *Plan Your Estate,* by Denis Clifford, offers in-depth coverage of all significant elements of estate planning, from simple wills to complex tax-saving trusts, from funerals to family businesses.
- *Quicken WillMaker & Trust* (software for Windows and Mac) helps you to prepare a comprehensive will, which includes naming a personal guardian for your young children, naming property managers for young beneficiaries, and naming a caretaker for your pet. You can also use *Quicken WillMaker & Trust* to prepare a living trust, a living will, durable powers of attorney for health care, and finances, a document setting out your wishes for final arrangements, and other useful legal forms.
- *Nolo's Online Will* allows you to make a full-feature will online, using an interactive program that does not require that you buy or download software. With *Nolo's Online Will*, you can make your will quickly, for a minimum cost. Access the will at www.nolo.com/products/wills-trusts.
- *Quick & Legal Will Book,* by Denis Clifford, shows you how to prepare a basic will efficiently using documents downloaded to your computer.
- *Make Your Own Living Trust,* by Denis Clifford, provides a complete explanation of how to prepare a living trust. The book contains forms and information that show you how to create individual living trusts, shared living trusts, and basic wills.
- *Special Needs Trusts: Protect Your Child's Financial Future,* by Kevin Urbatsch and Michele Fuller-Urbatsch, gives you all the information and forms you need to create a trust that provides for a person with a disability without jeopardizing eligibility for government benefits.

- *Saving the Family Cottage: A Guide to Succession Planning for Your Cottage, Cabin, Camp or Vacation Home,* by Stuart Hollander, Rose Hollander, and David S. Fry, explains succession planning for a vacation home, covering issues that can arise with shared ownership, from choosing the right legal entity for that home to renting it.
- *8 Ways to Avoid Probate,* by Mary Randolph, offers a thorough discussion of all the major ways to transfer property at death without probate.
- *The Executor's Guide: Settling a Loved One's Estate or Trust,* by Mary Randolph, is a comprehensive handbook to help executors and trustees wind up a deceased person's affairs. It can also help you get your estate in shape for your own executor or trustee.
- *The Trustee's Legal Companion,* by Liza Hanks and Carol Elias Zolla, presents a comprehensive explanation of serving as a trustee of a living trust, including state-by-state charts of all relevant laws.
- *Get It Together: Organize Your Records So Your Family Won't Have To,* by Melanie Cullen, with Shae Irving, provides a complete system you can use to organize your legal documents, financial records, and other important personal information for your executor and other loved ones.
- *How to Probate an Estate in California,* by Julia Nissley and Lisa Fialco, shows how to probate an uncomplicated California estate without an attorney.
- *Living Wills & Powers of Attorney for California,* by Shae Irving, enables California residents to prepare health care and financial incapacity documents.
- *Long-Term Care: How to Plan & Pay for It,* by Joseph L. Matthews, is a practical guide that provides all the information you need to help make the best arrangements for long-term care. It shows how to protect assets, arrange home health care, find nursing- and non–nursing-home residences, evaluate nursing home insurance, and understand Medicare, Medicaid, and other benefit programs.

- *Social Security, Medicare & Government Pensions: Get the Most Out of Your Retirement & Medical Benefits,* by Joseph L. Matthews, shows you the way through the current maze of rights and benefits for those 55 and over, including Medicare, Medicaid, and Social Security retirement and disability benefits, as well as age-discrimination protections.
- *Nolo's Guide to Social Security Disability: Getting & Keeping Your Benefits,* by David A. Morton, helps you understand who is eligible for Social Security disability benefits and shows you how to get any benefits that are due to you.

You can find all of these resources on www.nolo.com. There, you'll also find lots of free legal information on a wide range of topics, including plenty of material to help you plan your estate. ●

Your Beneficiaries

H ere we reach the core of estate planning: deciding who will receive your property after you die. This can be a satisfying part of the estate planning process because you can contemplate the benefits your property will bring to the people or organizations you choose. When it comes to naming beneficiaries, you are free to make whatever decisions you wish, except that if you are married, in most states you must leave at least half of your property to your spouse.

For estate planning purposes, beneficiaries can be divided into two groups, depending on the rights you give them. "Direct beneficiaries" receive your property outright. "Alternate beneficiaries" receive property only if the direct beneficiary for that gift is not alive when you die. Below we'll take a closer look at beneficiary types, as well as possible beneficiary complexities.

Direct Beneficiaries

A direct beneficiary is a person or institution you name in a will, trust, or pay-on-death account to receive a gift of specific property. For example, if you leave your car to your daughter, she is a direct beneficiary. You can have as many different direct beneficiaries, for different gifts, as you choose.

Definition: Gifts

You leave your beneficiaries some type of property. I call this leaving them a gift. Lawyers often use words like "bequest" or "legacy." (The latter defined by Ambrose Bierce as "a gift from one legging it out of this vale of tears.") Of course, the word "gift" can also be used to mean property freely given from one living person to another, or to an organization. (For more information, see "Making Gifts During Life," in Chapter 10.)

Direct beneficiaries come in two types:

- primary beneficiaries—people or institutions named to receive specifically identified property, and
- residuary beneficiaries—people or organizations named to receive any property not specifically left to primary beneficiaries.

EXAMPLE: In her will Kira leaves her car to her friend Alice, her jewelry to her friend Dori, and $10,000 to the Sierra Club. All these are direct primary beneficiaries. She leaves all other property subject to her will to her brother Tom. He is her direct residuary beneficiary.

CAUTION

Special rule for Floridians. The Florida Constitution (Art. 10, § 4) prohibits the head of a family from leaving a family residence to someone other than a spouse or minor child, if either exists. See a lawyer if you have questions about how this law applies to you.

As mentioned in Chapter 1, many people's beneficiary situations are relatively simple. Even if you want to name many different beneficiaries for different specific items of property, your beneficiary plan can still be simple. As long as you clearly set out which person gets which item, there should be no trouble. Other people, however, don't have it so easy. Complicated questions may arise about possible beneficiaries. But before discussing these complexities, let's look at one concern you should address no matter what your beneficiary situation: whether to name alternate beneficiaries.

Gifts to Caregivers in California, Illinois, or Nevada

If you live in California, Illinois, or Nevada and want to leave a substantial gift to any nonrelative who has recently helped you with personal or health care, see a lawyer first. You can leave such a gift—but first you may need to have a lawyer sign a statement, verifying that you're acting freely and aren't being unduly influenced.

If you don't, the gift could be void—meaning the intended recipient won't get it. These states have laws that aim to prevent caregivers from taking advantage of the people who depend on them. However, the laws could easily invalidate perfectly reasonable gifts that you really want to make. For example, a gift to a new neighbor who brings meals and helps you pay bills could be voided, as could a gift to a paid live-in caregiver who has become a good friend.

These laws apply only to gifts greater than:

- $5,000 in California (or less if your entire estate will be worth less than $166,250)
- $20,000 in Illinois, and
- $3,000 in Nevada.

Most gifts to family members won't be affected, but gifts to loved ones who are not legally related, like stepchildren or unmarried partners, could be voided if your will is challenged.

If you think these laws could void gifts that you want to make, see a lawyer who handles estate planning, family law, or elder care matters for help.

(Cal. Prob. Code §§ 21380-21392, 755 Ill. Comp. Stat. Ann. § 5/4a, Nev. Rev. Stat. §§ 155.093-155.098.)

Alternate Beneficiaries

An alternate beneficiary is a person or organization you name to receive a gift you left to a direct beneficiary, if that direct beneficiary dies before you, or does not outlive you by a defined period of time, often 30 to 45 days. (This is called a "survivorship requirement.") You can name one or more alternate beneficiaries for every one of your direct beneficiaries. Commonly, spouses who leave all of their property to each other name their children as alternate beneficiaries. Other alternate beneficiary plans can be more complex.

> **EXAMPLE:** Howard decides to leave his property equally to his brother, Al, and sister, Sheila. Howard also decides that if Al dies before him, Al's share of the property should be divided as follows: 25% each to Al's three children, and 25% to named charities. If Sheila dies before Howard, he divides her share this way: 50% to her daughter, 25% to named charities, and the remaining 25% to a political cause.

When preparing your will or living trust, should you name alternate beneficiaries? The conventional estate planning advice is that you should—indeed must. I disagree. Generally, naming alternate beneficiaries is wise, but it's not necessary to name them in every situation.

If there's a reasonable chance that a primary beneficiary will not outlive you, for instance if the beneficiary is elderly or ill, it's surely sensible to name an alternate. Of course, you could amend your will or trust to name a new beneficiary for property left to someone who predeceases you, but naming alternates will save you the work. Also, it eliminates the risk that you won't be able to amend your will or living trust—or that you simply won't get around to it. Better to name alternative beneficiaries so that you have a plan in place from the get-go.

So why would someone decide not to name alternate beneficiaries? Because naming alternate beneficiaries means considering a horrible event—someone you love dying before you do.

> **EXAMPLE:** Demitrous, a widower, leaves all of his property to his daughter, Irene. He refuses to contemplate her dying before him, and does not name an alternate beneficiary. The risk is that if she does predecease him, and he doesn't name a new beneficiary, his property will be distributed to his closest relatives according to state law, which might not be what he wished.

The example above is an extreme case, because there is only one beneficiary and no backup. Most people don't put all their eggs in one basket, so a more serious question is how far down the route of alternate beneficiaries they want to go. For instance, do you want to make a plan for what happens to a gift if both the direct and alternate beneficiaries die before you? What if all your children and grandchildren die before you?

I have six brothers and sisters, all healthy. My parents prepared a shared living trust in their early 70s. Each decided that they wanted to leave all their property to the other spouse. Also, each chose to name all seven children as equal alternate beneficiaries, so that when one spouse died, the children would become the direct beneficiaries of the surviving spouse.

My parents did not want to name alternates to their children. I understood their decision. Neither wanted to imagine one of their children dying before both of them, and I certainly wasn't going to try to talk them into such morbid speculation.

Of course, some people want to carry out several levels of beneficiary planning, naming alternates for each alternate and so on. That's fine too. An important purpose of estate planning is to give you peace of mind that, as far as worldly property goes, you've prepared for the consequences of your death. If you are comforted by knowing that your planning includes what happens to your property if there are multiple tragedies, do that planning. The bottom line is that, as with all your basic estate planning decisions, you are your own expert, and you can decide what feels right.

Beneficiary Complexities

Viewed pragmatically, estate planning is a mix of property, deep human emotions, and law. The legal devices themselves should not be intimidating. As I've urged, you can master them well enough to do your own basic planning. It's the blend of property and emotions that can cause serious problems. Money may not be *the* root of all evil, but it's high on the list. Of course, few people worry about evil when doing their planning. But many are concerned with how to distribute their property fairly, or how to prevent, as best they can, future conflicts over that property.

Ultimately, these are personal matters, not to be left to estate planners—certainly not me. However, I can offer some examples of beneficiary complexities and solutions drawn from the real life (sometimes, too-real life) of my estate planning practice.

Second or Subsequent Marriages

As noted, "blended" families, or sometimes not-so-blended families, can raise complex and difficult estate planning concerns. Individual situations can vary greatly, often depending on whether marriages occurred relatively early or late in life and on how well family members get along. But one thing is obvious—if yours is a blended family, you must carefully consider, and do your best to reconcile, needs that may be competing and conflicting.

A common problem is how to provide for your current spouse while still keeping the bulk of your property intact for your children from a previous marriage. A trust can be very useful here. (See "Marital Property Control Trusts for Second or Subsequent Marriages," in Chapter 11.)

Unmarried Couples

Unmarried couples usually have no automatic legal right to inherit each other's property. (The exceptions for registered domestic partners are discussed below.) A central concern of most members of unmarried couples is to arrange to leave property to the other. Happily, unmarried people have the right to leave their property to whomever they want, using a will or other transfer device like a living trust. In case of serious threat by hostile family members, a member of a couple may take action to establish by clear proof that she or he was mentally competent when the estate plan was prepared.

> EXAMPLE: Ernest and Arthur have lived together for many years. Aside from a few small gifts to friends or family, each wants to leave all property to the other after death. They're concerned with efficiency and economy, but above all they want to be sure that their estate plan can't be successfully attacked by several close relatives who have long been hostile to their relationship. Ernest and Arthur each prepare a living trust leaving their property as they desire. They videotape their signing and the notarization of this document, and have two witnesses watch them sign, to provide additional proof that they were both mentally competent and not under duress or undue influence when they finalized their documents.

Same-Sex Couples

If you have a same-sex partner, it's important to consider the legal status of your relationship when estate planning because it affects inheritance rights, tax issues, government benefits, the right to direct health care decisions, and more.

For many years, a turbulent legal landscape made it difficult for same-sex couples to keep track of their benefits and obligations related to marriage. Happily, that has changed, much for the better. In June 2015, the United States Supreme Court's decision in *Obergefell v. Hodges* made same-sex marriage legal in every state. Now, not only can same-sex couples get married anywhere in the United States, but they can also be sure that every state will recognize their marriage, regardless of which state issued the marriage license.

Further, couples in a same-sex marriage now have the right to receive the same marriage-related benefits that all married couples receive. For example, you can file your taxes jointly, you can receive insurance benefits through your spouse's employer, and you have a right to inherit part of your spouse's estate. You'll find detailed information about the rights and benefits of marriage in the Marriage Law section of Nolo.com at www. nolo.com/legal-encyclopedia/marriage-license. And as you read this book, you can assume that all discussions about marriage equally apply to marriages between people of the same sex.

A few states continue to recognize registered domestic partnerships in addition to same-sex marriage. In most cases, domestic partnerships provide many of the state rights and benefits of marriage, but they have no effect on federal issues. Keep in mind that a several states have converted their domestic partnerships to marriage—either automatically or by choice. If you live in one of those states, you may now be married even though you were issued a license for a domestic partnership. If you have any questions about the legal status of your relationship, contact a local family law attorney or your state's marriage equality organization for help.

RESOURCE
Learn more about the rights of same-sex couples. For thorough discussions of marriage and other legal and practical issues, see *Making It Legal: A Guide to Same-Sex Marriage, Domestic Partnerships and Civil Unions* and *A Legal Guide for Lesbian & Gay Couples*, both by Frederick Hertz and Emily Doskow. For free information online, go to the LGBT Law section of Nolo.com at www.nolo.com/legal-encyclopedia/lgbt-law.

Unequal Distribution of Property

Parents, or a parent, may want to leave property unequally between two or more children. This is perfectly legal. The problem may be what the kids think and feel about it.

> EXAMPLE 1: Gunnar and Louise are married, with a modest estate. They have two children in their twenties: Andrea, in her first year of medical school, and Suzanne, who's happily married to a rich man. Each spouse leaves all his or her property to the other. The alternate beneficiaries, who will receive the property when both spouses die, are their children.
>
> Gunnar and Louise decide that they will leave 75% of their property to Andrea, who faces many more years of financial strain before she becomes a surgeon. But the couple is also aware that they may need to revise their plan after Andrea achieves her goal, or if Suzanne encounters financial stresses. Also, they decide they want to explain their decisions to both daughters, to see if they agree that the plan is fair.

> EXAMPLE 2: Sherry has three children: Patricia, a prosperous lawyer, Albert, a successful journalist, and Caroline, a dancer and single mother. Sherry decides she will leave most of her estate to Caroline, because she's the only child who really needs financial help. Sherry decides to talk to all three children together, to discuss what percentage to leave to each child, and the circumstances under which she'd change her property distribution.

These are nice tidy examples, but reality may be more murky. Perhaps children who receive less than an equal portion will feel disturbed or resentful. Perhaps not every conflict can be resolved by one amicable discussion. Sometimes, a major part of estate planning is facing that there are serious conflicts between your beneficiaries, or even within you, about the distribution of your property.

Shared Gifts

You can name more than one beneficiary for a gift. Indeed, you can name as many beneficiaries as you want to share a gift.

When naming shared beneficiaries, you need to resolve two key questions. First, what does each beneficiary receive? This is normally handled by leaving percentages of the gift to each recipient.

> EXAMPLE: "I leave my house to my children as follows:
> 35% to Alexis
> 25% to Constance
> 25% to Edward
> 15% to Phyllis."

Next, you need to decide if the gift should be sold promptly after you die and the proceeds divided between the beneficiaries in the percentages you specified, or if your beneficiaries are to share ongoing ownership of the property. This latter alternative raises some thorny problems—for example, how will the beneficiaries share control or management of the asset, and what will happen if one or more beneficiaries wants to sell? You must consider possible conflicts between your beneficiaries—not abstract possibilities of conflict, which always exist short of paradise, but difficulties that might actually occur. In William Butler Yeats's phrase, "cast a cold eye" on the characters and relationships of your beneficiaries. A gift with continuing shared ownership is a good idea only if you are confident that there won't be significant conflict among them.

> EXAMPLE: Lewis wants to leave the family house equally to his three adult children. He doesn't want them to sell the house because one child, Joe, who's had money and work problems, lives there for free. But Lewis also knows that another child feels Joe is a moocher and needs to grow up. Also, Lewis doesn't want to let Joe live in the house forever for free, depriving the other two children of their inheritance. Lewis needs to resolve whether he

really wants to leave the house with continuing shared ownership, or simply order it sold, and possibly leave more than one-third of the proceeds to Joe.

> **SEE AN EXPERT**
>
> **Getting help for continuing shared ownership.** If you want to leave a gift that involves ongoing shared ownership, see a lawyer to work out the terms and form of that ownership. You might want to provide some rules to govern ownership, including possible disputes. Leaving the property in a trust can be an effective way to create binding rules, but this kind of trust requires careful professional drafting.

Long-Term Care for a Child With Special Needs

Parents of children with mental or physical disabilities may need to provide for the future care and support for those children whether they are minors or adults. To achieve this goal, many parents create long-term trusts (often called "special needs trusts") that protect the children and the children's assets even after the parents die. The purpose of the trust is to provide for a child with a disability without jeopardizing the child's eligibility for government benefits. Because the child does not legally own the trust assets, those assets do not count when determining eligibility. An independent trustee can spend trust income or principal for a wide variety of the child's needs that are not covered by government benefits. *Special Needs Trusts: Protect Your Child's Financial Future*, by Kevin Urbatsch and Michelle Fuller-Urbatsch (Nolo), explains these trusts and provides the information and forms you need to create one. (For more information, see "Special Needs Trusts for People With Disabilities," in Chapter 11.)

Some parents decide to concentrate most of their resources on their child with a disability, leaving less for any other children, as illustrated by the following example.

EXAMPLE: The Balfour family has a child with serious disabilities, Bob, age 15, who will need care all his life. They have two other children, both of whom are healthy. The Balfours' primary estate planning concern is doing all they can to arrange for Bob's care after they die. They realize this means leaving Bob most of their modest estate. They discuss this with their 19-year-old daughter, Rebecca, who says that's fine. Their 17-year-old son, Jeb, resents the attention Bob gets and isn't so acquiescent. But the Balfours decide that protecting Bob remains their top priority. They hope that, as Jeb matures, he will understand the difficulties Bob faces and that his resentment of Bob will fade.

There are many questions the parents must resolve about Bob. Who will be responsible for his personal care after they die? How can they best leave money for Bob's use? How will any money they leave be treated when determining eligibility for government benefits? After all, it makes no sense to leave money to Bob if it means he will be ineligible for government help until it's all used up. The Balfours must choose a personal guardian to be responsible for Bob until he becomes a legal adult at age 18. They must also choose a financial guardian who will manage the money they leave for Bob during Bob's lifetime.

The Balfours discuss these concerns themselves and then broaden their discussion to include Rebecca, other family members, and close friends they are considering for these two tasks. Eventually, they choose Mrs. Balfour's younger sister to be Bob's personal guardian, if needed. They name their closest friend, William, to be Bob's financial manager, until Rebecca turns 30. After that, she will become Bob's financial manager.

To understand how to dovetail money they leave Bob in trust with government benefits, the Balfours do some preliminary research. They decide to establish a special needs trust for Bob. Using Nolo's *Special Needs Trusts*, they draft a trust that protects Bob's eligibility for government assistance programs and gives the trustee (the property manager) control over trust property to use for Bob's benefit.

Irresponsible Beneficiaries

Some people worry that if they leave property directly to an adult beneficiary, the beneficiary will squander the money. The usual way to handle
this concern is to leave property to the beneficiary in a trust. A trustee
who is not the beneficiary handles the property and distributes it to the
beneficiary as the trust directs. (In Chapter 11, see "Spendthrift Trusts.")

Placing Controls on Gifts

For various reasons, you may be tempted to try to impose controls on your
gifts, rather than leaving them outright to beneficiaries. For example, if
you want your gift to stay in the family or if you want a beneficiary to
get a gift only under certain conditions, you may hope to use your estate
plan to control that property after you die. However, such "dead-hand"
controls are usually not a good idea. In fact, some are not legal, some just
aren't feasible, and many can cause real problems with your estate plan.
First, you should know that you can't legally control your property for
many generations. The basic legal rule is that you can impose controls
for a maximum period of "lives in being" (that is, people alive now) plus
21 years. Further, some controls are too difficult to enforce. For example,
suppose you leave a gift to someone only if he quits smoking. Who is to
police that person? For how long must he quit smoking? What happens
if he doesn't? Trying to impose moral requirements on your beneficiaries
simply won't work.

This just scratches the surface of how difficult it is to try to control
someone's behavior in any way after your death. (Indeed, it's hard enough
to have any control while you're alive.) Except for trusts for minors (see
Chapter 3) and a couple of standard property control trusts (discussed in
Chapter 11), it's wiser to accept that you can't shape others' actions once
you're in the grave than it is to spend a lot of money for a lawyer-drafted
trust that merely offers the illusion that you can. After all, Louis XIV tried
to do it, and those controls were ignored promptly after his death. If the
"Sun King" was unable to control behavior from his grave, who can?

SEE AN EXPERT

Don't try to do it yourself. If you're determined to control the behavior of your beneficiaries after you die, see a lawyer. And be prepared to spend some money; the trusts you will need are complicated and costly.

Pets as Beneficiaries

Although pets may seem like part of the family, legally, pets are property. This means you can't leave money or property directly to your pets because they can't own things. But you can try to ensure that your pet will continue to have a good life after you're gone. The easiest thing to do is to arrange with a friend or family member to care for your pet. Then in your will or living trust, you leave your pet to that person, along with money that will be needed to care for your pet.

> EXAMPLE: Gina has an eight-year-old black lab named Buddy. She's concerned about what would happen to Buddy if she were to die unexpectedly. So she talks to her sister, who agrees to take care of Buddy if Gina becomes unable to do so. She also does some math and figures out that she spends about $500 a year on Buddy's food, supplies, and medical care. Then, in her will, Gina leaves Buddy to her sister, along with $7,000 to cover Buddy's expenses for the rest of his life.

 SEE AN EXPERT

See an attorney for a pet trust. The laws of every state and the District of Columbia allow pet owners to set up trusts for their pets. A pet trust allows you to place some requirements on the new owner of your pet (like about how to care for your pet), whereas a will passes your pet to a new owner with no strings attached. If you want to create a pet trust, you'll need help from a lawyer.

Simultaneous Death

Many couples, especially those with small children, are concerned about what will happen if both die at the same time. Sure, they know that this is highly unlikely, but that doesn't negate the genuine worry.

With young children, the person named by both parents as the children's personal guardian steps in to raise the children. (Each member of a couple should choose the same adult as personal guardian; this is discussed at the beginning of Chapter 3.)

Distributing property can be problematic in simultaneous death because couples often leave their property to each other. What happens if one spouse lives five minutes longer than the other? Does all of that spouse's property go to the beneficiaries of the spouse that lived longer? Or suppose it can't be determined which spouse outlived the other? What is the best way to ensure that property is left the way each spouse intended?

Here are two methods that can be used to make sure each spouse's property wishes are followed:

- A "survivorship clause" is imposed over all gifts, including those to a spouse, requiring each beneficiary to outlive the giver by a set period, often 30 or 45 days. If the beneficiary does not survive this period, the gift goes to the alternate beneficiary.
- Each spouse's will and living trust contains a "simultaneous death clause," which provides that when it's difficult or impossible to tell which spouse died first, the property of each spouse is disposed of as if he or she had survived the other.

Logically inclined readers may wonder how this can work. How can I be presumed to have survived my wife when she's presumed to have survived me? Yes, it's a paradox, but it's allowed because it works to get the desired results. Technically, the argument is that each spouse's property is handled independently of the other. In reality, as the oft-cited quote of Oliver Wendell Holmes explains, "The life of the law has not been logic, it has been experience."

EXAMPLE: Guillermo and Venus are killed in a plane crash. Each had a will leaving all property to the other. Guillermo's alternate beneficiaries are his brother and sister. Venus's alternate beneficiary is her daughter from her first marriage. Each will contains a simultaneous death clause. For property distribution purposes, Guillermo's will is treated as if he survived Venus, so his property goes to his brother and sister. Similarly, Venus's will is treated as if she survived Guillermo, so her property goes to her daughter.

Disinheritance

You have no legal duty to leave anyone property, except that in common law states, you must leave property to your spouse. (See "A Spouse's Right to Inherit Property," in Chapter 1.) Also, except for your children, you don't have to expressly disinherit others; anyone not mentioned in your will has no right to any of your property.

You have the legal right to disinherit any child but you must clearly express that intention in your will. Most states have laws to protect children of any age from being accidentally disinherited. If a child is neither named in your will nor specifically disinherited, these laws provide that the child has a right to a portion of your estate. In most states, these laws apply only to children born after you made your will, but in a few states they apply to any child. Further, in some states, these laws apply not only to children but to any child of a child who has died. For this reason, if you want to disinherit a child or grandchild, it's critical that you state this explicitly in your will. You can do this by either stating your intention ("I leave my son Michael nothing") or by listing all your children and grandchildren and then leaving nothing to those whom you intend to disinherit.

Lawsuits Against Your Estate

Some people worry that their will or living trust will be legally challenged by a disgruntled would-be inheritor, or a beneficiary who didn't get what he or she expected. First of all, it's important to realize that this rarely happens. Almost all wills and trusts are handled without lawsuits. Also, no one but your spouse (and a child not expressly disinherited) has a legal right to any of your property. Still, some people fear that there are so many technicalities to a will or living trust that's it's difficult to get it done right, at least without paying a small fortune to a lawyer. This simply isn't true. Wills and living trusts have a few formalities, but only a few. With proper instructions and well-drafted forms, it's not a big deal to get it done right.

Others worry that, even if technically sound, their will or living trust could be invalidated in court. This also is not true. A court will invalidate a will or living trust only if it finds that the person who made it was mentally incompetent, or that the document was made under fraud or duress. An example of fraud is giving someone a paper to sign that the signer thinks is a letter, but is actually a will. Duress means convincing someone to sign a document using pressure or coercion.

Fraud or duress are hard to prove, even when they actually happen. They are almost impossible to prove if they didn't happen. Of course, under our legal system, it's not hard to file a lawsuit challenging a will or trust. These days, you can find a lawyer to file just about anything. But a frivolous lawsuit is not cause for big worry, though it may indeed be some hassle to your inheritors.

SEE AN EXPERT

If you fear a lawsuit. If you think anyone might file a lawsuit against your will or living trust, see a lawyer. With an attorney's help, you can take steps to diminish the chances that a lawsuit would be successful.

Talking It Over

You may want to talk about your estate plans with close family members or other key beneficiaries, in the hope of making property transfer smoother after you die. Talking things over can be as simple as telling your beneficiaries what you've done. Or you can expand your discussions, and take your beneficiaries into the planning process.

Consider Discussing Your Plan

In my view, if you think you can safely discuss what you've done with your closest family members or other prime beneficiaries, it's a very good idea to do so. After all, they'll find out eventually, so why keep it a secret now? I know families where serious emotional damage was done—or compounded—by keeping estate planning secrets. One friend, who'd been raised in near-poverty and whose parents continued to live a life of penury, was shocked and hurt (as well as pleased) when he learned that his inheritance was over $400,000.

Even in less extreme situations, keeping your plans a secret may raise serious questions. Why the need for secrecy? If there's something troubling or difficult that may need to be faced, consider dealing with it while you live—and can have some input into things. On the other hand, communication is not always a cure-all. If, after reflection, you decide that you don't want to reveal your plan—well, it *is* your plan, and (to stress it yet again) there aren't any must-do rules here.

Ethical Wills: Leaving Your Thoughts Behind

An "ethical will" is a document or materials in which a person expresses the beliefs and experiences that have mattered the most in his or her life. This statement can have real value both to those close to you and to future generations.

If creating an ethical will sounds like a good idea to you, it's better to put it in a document separate from your main estate planning documents. Summing up what's in your soul may take pages. Better not to enmesh that profound searching with the practical job of a will or trust.

Talking as Part of the Planning Process

Some people decide to include close beneficiaries in their planning process. Among other benefits, this may help you clarify your decisions.

> **EXAMPLE:** A couple of my siblings have done, as it's said, "very well." And my parents, though far from rich, wound up, through decades of prudence and hard work, with an estate far larger then they'd imagined. One prosperous brother generously suggested to my mother that they not leave him any money, because he had plenty. My mother asked what I thought. I'd learned from estate planning clients that my job often included helping them discern what they really wanted, not instructing them. After I'd posed a few questions to my mother about how she really felt (rather than what was abstractly "right"), she became clear that she wanted to leave equal shares to all her children. She loved each, and felt that leaving unequal shares might create an impression that she loved some more than others. I concurred, adding that I had chosen to be a renegade legal writer rather than an affluent corporate lawyer. Why should I get more than my brother because I had made what was, for me, a good choice?

From another perspective, part of the satisfaction of estate planning can be asking those you love what specific items of yours they want. Further, perhaps you'll be fortunate and there will be no conflicts over heirlooms—but if there are, you can resolve them now, while you're alive.

> **EXAMPLE:** My frugal mother somehow managed to purchase a number of fine etchings during the 1940s and 1950s. Rather than simply leave them for the kids to divide up after her death, my mother asked us to go through them and select at least one that we each wanted. This was not a tightly structured process. During a visit to our old home, one or another of us would look at the etchings and choose. There was some overlap of choices, but nothing we couldn't work out.
>
> Through her giving, my mother not only had the pleasure of anticipating who would have which etching, but she's also had the fun of going through them several times, and going through them with children who've loved at least some of them since childhood. ●

Children

I n estate planning, the word "children" can have two meanings. The first is "minors"—individuals who are not yet 18. The second meaning is offspring of any age; parents who live long enough can have "children" who are in their 40s, 50s, or even older. This chapter focuses primarily on minor children because that's such a vital concern for so many parents. I also briefly discuss ways to leave property to a young adult child, when you're concerned that the child may not be sufficiently mature to handle money responsibly. Finally, I cover leaving property to other people's children.

Most parents of minor children are understandably concerned with what will happen to their children if disaster strikes and the parents die. If both parents are raising the children, this concern usually centers on simultaneous death of the parents. If you're a single parent and the other parent is deceased, has abandoned the child, or is unavailable for some other reason, the worry is what will happen to your child if you die before the child reaches adulthood.

Naming Someone to Care for Young Children

If a child has two capable parents and one dies, normally the other parent has the legal right to assume sole custody. Even if the parents are divorced or never married, as long as both parents are participating in raising their children, this rule presents no problem. But what happens if both parents die? Or a sole parent dies? Or a custodial parent believes the other should never have custody of the children?

First, some legal rules. Every minor must be raised by an adult who is legally responsible for the child's care. If there are no parents capable of handling this responsibility, another adult, called the child's "personal guardian," will be appointed by a court. In your will, you can nominate someone to be your child's personal guardian, and a backup, called the successor personal guardian. If you have young children, this is a major reason why a will is essential.

The person you name as personal guardian cannot actually serve as the legal guardian until approved by a court. The judge has the authority to name someone else if the judge is convinced it is in the best interests of the child. This may seem outrageous to you—how could a judge have authority to go against your own choice of the best guardian for your child? The short, legal answer is that children are not property and cannot simply be "left" to someone as a diamond bracelet or an automobile can be. That said, the reality is that if, as is usually the case, no one contests your choice for your child's personal guardian, a court will almost certainly confirm the person you choose. In practice, a court will reject an unopposed nominee only if there are grave and provable reasons to do so, such as a serious criminal background, child abuse, or dangerous self-destructiveness, such as drug addiction.

Revise Your Estate Plan to Include New Children

If, after preparing your estate plan, you have or adopt a new child, revise that plan by providing for her or him. Naturally, you'll want to do this. But if somehow you don't get around to it, that child has a legal right to inherit a portion of your property. (See "Disinheritance," in Chapter 2.) The percentage of your estate that this child would take by law might not be what you desire. And a legally mandated inheritance could upset your estate plan in other ways. For example, you might want your new child, along with other children, to be an alternate beneficiary, with no inheritance rights if your primary beneficiaries survive you. Whatever your wishes, it's better to revise your plan and put them in writing.

Choosing Your Child's Personal Guardian

You may well know whom you want to name as your child's personal guardian. For many parents, there's one obvious choice—an adult who is willing to take on the responsibility and would love and care for the child. Other parents have to struggle to decide on a personal guardian. Sometimes two parents don't initially agree on who is the best choice. And other times, both for couples and single parents, there appears to be no fully satisfactory choice. But however you get there, you do need to make a decision—and then resume living with the faith that the person you named will never need to serve. You should always name a successor personal guardian as well, in case your first choice is unable to serve or to continue to serve.

You can name one guardian for all of your children, or name different guardians for each of your children. Your choice will likely depend on the relationships your children have with their other parent, each other, and the potential guardians. If your children are close in age and have similar relationships with family members who are potential guardians, naming one guardian for all of your kids may be a good choice. However, if your children are far apart in age or have strong relationships with different family members, then you may find that it makes the most sense to name different guardians for each of your children. Keep in mind that a judge will make the final decision about what is best for each child. So it may be a good idea to attach a statement to your will setting out why you've chosen the guardians you have. A court isn't required to follow this statement, or even accept it as valid evidence, but a conscientious judge will surely consider it.

EXAMPLE: Janine has custody of her two daughters, aged 14 and 15, from her first marriage, and her son, age 6, from her second. Her first husband has never taken any interest in or responsibility for the girls. Her second ex, Todd, has been an adequate, though from Janine's view, well below superb, father to their son, and has also tried to be decent to her daughters. Though the three children would like to stay together, Janine reluctantly recognizes that this can't be paramount in her decision. Janine's sister, Brenda, is close to the daughters and Janine strongly believes that she would be a much better personal guardian for them than Todd. But Todd would certainly want and be entitled to custody of their son.

Janine names Brenda as guardian for her daughters. She also names Brenda to serve as successor guardian for her son if neither she nor Todd is alive. Then, she names Todd as successor guardian for the girls. She also attaches a statement to her will explaining why she believes this arrangement is best for her children.

If You Don't Want the Other Parent to Become Personal Guardian

One parent might not want the other parent to have custody for any of a number of reasons. For example, a parent might believe that his child's other parent is dangerously destructive, emotionally or physically. Or, a remarried parent might believe that her current spouse would be a far better guardian for her child than her ex, the child's biological father.

Clearly, one parent should not lightly attempt to deprive the other of custody. But strong reasons may compel a custodial parent to nominate someone other than the child's other parent to be personal guardian. In that case, what happens if the custodial parent dies and the custody issue is presented to a judge? There is no definitive answer. If the other parent doesn't contest the deceased parent's wishes, the court will almost surely follow those wishes. ("Almost surely" is as certain as you ever get when it comes to courts.) But if the parent contests custody, a judge's decision would turn on both the facts of the situation and the judge's own beliefs. Generally, a court will not appoint someone other than a biological or legal parent unless that parent:

- is unavailable
- has legally abandoned the child, or
- is an unfit parent.

It's usually quite difficult to prove that a parent is unfit, absent severe problems such as serious drug abuse, a history of violence to the child, or mental illness.

It's unlikely that anyone except the child's other parent would win custody against your wishes. For instance, if you name your best friend, Betty, to raise your children if you can't, and Betty is clearly a caring adult, it's unlikely that someone else, such as the child's grandmother or uncle, could gain custody over your choice.

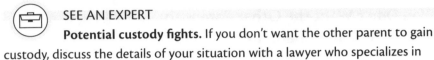

SEE AN EXPERT

Potential custody fights. If you don't want the other parent to gain custody, discuss the details of your situation with a lawyer who specializes in family law.

Naming Someone to Manage Your Child's Property

Minor children cannot own property outright, free of adult control, beyond a minimal amount—usually between $2,500 and $5,000, depending on the state. So, if you leave property to your minor child (whether as direct or alternate beneficiary), you must name an adult to be legally responsible for managing that property until the child becomes an adult. For now, let's call this adult your child's "property manager." You should also name a successor property manager, in case your first choice can't serve.

In contrast to a personal guardian, your choices for property manager and alternate property manager are normally binding and not subject to court review. This is because a property manager controls only money and property, which you have a right to leave as you want.

Leaving Property to Your Spouse for the Benefit of Your Children

One option for parents of young children is for each to leave property outright to the other spouse to be used for their children's benefit. This approach makes sense if the parents trust each other, but obviously it isn't desirable if the other parent is not available or is financially imprudent. Even if you leave all property to your spouse, it's always wise to name a property manager for your child. This ensures that the person you've chosen will manage your child's property if you and your spouse die simultaneously.

Using Life Insurance to Provide for Your Children

If you have young children but not much money, term life insurance can provide cash to support your children if you die while they are still young. Because term life insurance pays benefits only if you die during the covered period (often five or ten years), it's far cheaper than other types of life insurance. (For more information, see "Naming Children as Beneficiaries of Life Insurance," below.)

The duty of your child's property manager is to manage property you leave for your children, or any other valuable property they acquire, honestly and in the children's best interests. This means that the property manager should use it to pay for normal living expenses and health and education needs. If you pick someone with integrity and common sense, your child's property should be in good hands. If substantial funds are involved, the property manager can pay for help to handle the more technical aspects of financial management. For instance, it's routine for a property manager to turn complicated tax and accounting matters over to an accountant.

When deciding on your minor child's property manager, here's a sensible rule: Name the same person you choose as your child's personal guardian, unless there are compelling reasons to name someone else. For example, choose a different person if you're concerned that the personal guardian doesn't have sufficient financial or practical experience to manage property prudently. Similarly, for alternate property manager, name the same person you designated as the child's alternate personal guardian unless there are strong reasons to choose someone else.

Obviously, the property manager must be willing to do the job, which might, depending on the ages of your children, last for many years. It's also wise to choose someone the other members of your family respect and accept. You want your children to inherit money, not family arguments.

Except as a last resort, don't name a bank or other financial institution to be property manager. Most banks won't manage accounts they consider too small to be worth the bother; as a rough rule, this means accounts worth less than $250,000. And when they do agree to manage an account, they charge hefty fees for every little act. In addition, it's my experience that banks are simply too impersonal to properly meet your own child's needs. Far better to name a human being you trust than a bureaucracy.

Selecting Different Property Managers for Different Children

In some situations, you may want to name different property managers for different minor children. Doing this is legal and does not require court approval.

Choosing How Your Children's Property Should Be Managed

You can choose the way property you leave to your children will be managed. You have three basic options:

- a custodianship, under what's called the Uniform Transfers to Minors Act
- a trust, either an individual child's trust for each child or a combined family pot trust, or
- a property guardianship.

The Uniform Transfers to Minors Act

A convenient device for leaving property to your child, by will or living trust, is the Uniform Transfers to Minors Act (UTMA), a law that has been adopted by every state except South Carolina. Under the UTMA, your child's adult property manager is called a "custodian." You can choose any adult you want to be custodian. The custodian's management ends when the child reaches age 18 to 25, depending on state law.

Here's how leaving a gift using the UTMA works:

In either your will or living trust, you identify the property you want to leave to the minor, then name him or her as beneficiary (direct or alternate) for that gift. Then you name the adult custodian who would be responsible for supervising the property until the child reaches the age at which he will receive the property outright. The custodian is entitled to reasonable compensation for his or her services; this payment comes out of the gift property. You also name a "successor custodian" in case your first choice can't do the job.

> **EXAMPLE:** In her will, Pauline leaves $25,000 to her nephew Sacha. She completes an UTMA clause as follows: "All property I leave by my will to Sacha Pichiny shall be given to his father, Jules Pichiny, as custodian for Sacha Pichiny under the Uniform Transfers to Minors Act of New York."

No court supervision of the custodian is required. The UTMA gives the custodian broad discretion to control and use the property in the child's interest. Because the UTMA is built into state law, financial institutions know about it, which should make it easy for the custodian to carry out property management responsibilities. The custodian must keep records so that tax returns can be filed on behalf of the minor, but no separate tax return must be filed for the UTMA assets.

As a general rule, the less valuable the property involved, the more appropriate the UTMA is. If the property will likely be used up by the time the child turns 18, or for college costs, using the UTMA is sensible. For example, given current college costs, you might leave a gift between $50,000 to $200,000 using the UTMA in states where the beneficiary does not get property until he or she reaches 21 or 25.

Age Limits for the Uniform Transfers to Minors Act

State	Age at Which Minor Gets Property	State	Age at Which Minor Gets Property
Alabama	21	Missouri	21
Alaska	18 to 25	Montana	21
Arizona	21	Nebraska	21
Arkansas	18 to 21	Nevada	18 to 25
California	18 to 25	New Hampshire	21
Colorado	21	New Jersey	18 to 21
Connecticut	21	New Mexico	21
Delaware	21	New York	21
District of Columbia	18 to 21	North Carolina	18 to 21
Florida	21*	North Dakota	21
Georgia	21	Ohio	21 to 25
Hawaii	21	Oklahoma	18 to 21
Idaho	21	Oregon	21 to 25
Illinois	21	Pennsylvania	21 to 25
Indiana	21	Rhode Island	21
Iowa	21	South Dakota	18
Kansas	21	Tennessee	21 to 25
Kentucky	18	Texas	21
Louisiana	18	Utah	21
Maine	18 to 21	Vermont	21
Maryland	21	Virginia	18 to 21
Massachusetts	21	Washington	21 or 25
Michigan	18 to 21	West Virginia	21
Minnesota	21	Wisconsin	21
Mississippi	21	Wyoming	21 to 30

The UTMA has not been adopted in South Carolina. If you live in South Carolina, you can easily use a child's trust instead.

* In Florida, the minor can choose to receive UTMA funds at age 21, even if the account is set to terminate between ages 21 and 25.

Trusts for Children

A trust is a legal entity under which an adult, called a "trustee," has the responsibility of handling property in the trust for someone else, called the "trust beneficiary."

You can create a trust for your child in either your will or living trust. If you create a trust for your child in a will, then the trust property will include only the property that you leave to your child through your will. If you create a trust for your child in your living trust, then your child's trust will include only the property that you transferred to your living trust and named your child to receive.

With a child's trust, your child is the beneficiary, and your child's property manager is the trustee. The trust document sets out the trustee's responsibilities and the beneficiary's rights, and the age at which the beneficiary is entitled to receive the trust principal outright.

With a "family pot trust," the other major type of trust for children, two or more beneficiaries share rights to the principal of one trust. (There are also other, more sophisticated trusts that can be used for children, such as a "special needs" trust for a child with a disability, or a "spendthrift" trust for a child who simply can't handle money. See Chapter 11.)

Both a child's trust and a family pot trust are legal in all states. Like an UTMA custodianship, a child's trust or family pot trust can be established either by will or living trust. You select the adults you want to serve as trustee and successor trustee. The trustee is entitled to compensation paid from the trust property, as provided in the trust document. Usually, the document simply states that the trustee may be paid "reasonable compensation" for services rendered. Trying to pin down a specific rate, or otherwise strictly control how much the trustee is paid, indicates a mistrust of the trustee that should call into question whether a trust is desirable. If you don't completely trust your trustee, attempting to control the trustee through the trust document is unlikely to solve real problems.

With either type of trust, the trustee manages the trust property, under the terms of the trust document, until it is turned over to the beneficiary or beneficiaries. Normally, the trustee may use trust assets for the education, medical needs, and living expenses of a trust beneficiary.

How a Child's Trust Works

With a child's trust, you leave specified property to one child. If you have more than one child, you create a separate trust for each one, with the result that each child's trust property is managed independently. You choose the age at which the child will receive the trust property outright. Often, a parent requires the child to reach age 25, or 35, or even older, before she or he is entitled to the property. So a child's trust is commonly used when a large amount of money is left for a child—more than the $50,000 to $200,000 that is appropriate for an UTMA gift.

> **EXAMPLE:** Anita is a single mother of a ten-year-old, LuAnne. Anita wants to leave the house to LuAnne, but she does not want to risk LuAnne gaining legal control over the house until she is much older. So Anita leaves the house in a child's trust, names her brother as trustee, names her sister as the alternative trustee, and specifies that LuAnne will not receive the trust property outright until she is 35.

How a Family Pot Trust Works

With a family pot trust, you leave property collectively for two or more children in one common fund; any amount of trust property can be spent for any child. In other words, the trustee doesn't have to spend the same amount on each beneficiary. Usually, the trust ends when the youngest child becomes 18. A pot trust is most often used by parents with younger children. These parents want to keep family money together, capable of being spent on any child as needs require.

EXAMPLE: Sidney and Kim have three children, ages two, five, and seven. Each spouse leaves all his or her property to the other spouse, with all three children as alternate beneficiaries. Property is left to the children in a family pot trust. Sidney and Kim name Kim's brother Josh as trustee, and Josh's wife, Dianne, as successor trustee. If both Sidney and Kim die while any of their children are minors, all family funds will be available for the children as needed—as the money was when the parents lived.

Naming a Property Guardian

In your will, you can name a "property guardian," who has authority to manage any of your minor children's property that doesn't come with a built-in adult manager. For example, let's say you set up a child's trust for all of the property your child receives from you through your will. Then shortly after your death, your child directly inherits a sizable amount of money from an aunt. The trustee of your child's trust will have no power to manage the new inheritance because it is not in the child's trust and a judge will have to appoint someone to manage the inheritance. You can address this problem in your will by naming a property guardian who will look after any unexpected assets your child receives.

Using a property guardian should only be a back-up plan for property that you don't yet know about. It is rarely wise to use a property guardian as a plan for the management of specific property.

Here are several reasons:

- The property must go through your will, which means it is subject to probate. (See "Probate," in Chapter 5.)
- Property guardians are often subject to court review, reporting requirements, and strict rules as to how they can expend funds. All this usually requires hiring a lawyer and paying significant fees but does little to guarantee that the property manager will do a good job. And those lawyer's fees, of course, come out of the property left to benefit the minor.
- A property guardianship must end when the minor becomes 18.

Still, you should name a property guardian (and successor) in your will to handle any property that belongs to your young children and isn't covered by some other legal device. Specifically, naming a property guardian in your will provides a supervision mechanism in case your minor children:

- earn substantial money after you die, or
- receive a large gift or inheritance from someone else that doesn't itself name a property manager.

Naming a property guardian also provides management for any property you leave to your kids if you fail to include it in an UTMA custodianship, child's trust, or pot trust.

Naming Children as Beneficiaries of Life Insurance

For many parents—most commonly younger parents who haven't acquired substantial assets—life insurance is a major financial resource used to provide money for children in case one or both parents die. However, if you name your children as beneficiaries, or alternate beneficiaries, of your policy, and you die while the children are minors, the insurance company cannot legally turn over the proceeds directly to them. If you haven't arranged for an adult to supervise the proceeds, court proceedings will be necessary to appoint and supervise a property guardian. As discussed above, this is not a good idea. Here are your options for avoiding that hassle:

- Name the children as policy beneficiaries and name a custodian under the UTMA for the proceeds. Most insurance companies permit this and have forms for it.
- Leave the proceeds to your children using children's trusts or a family pot trust as part of a living trust. You name your living trust (or the trustee, if that's what the insurance company prefers) as the policy beneficiary. You'll need to give a copy of your living trust to the insurance company, as well as complete any other paperwork they require. Then, in your living trust, you name the children as beneficiaries for any insurance proceeds that trust receives. You also create, as part of your living trust, children's trusts or a family pot trust to impose adult management over that gift.

It may not be possible for you to use your will to leave insurance proceeds in a child's trust or pot trust. Some insurance companies balk at this, on the grounds the trust won't come into existence until you die, and the policy beneficiary must be in existence when named. Rather than try to persuade an insurance company that this can be done, it's better to use a living trust to achieve your goal.

Tax-Saving Accounts

Federal law provides for a few types of savings accounts that allow you to save for future education- or disability-related expenses with specific tax advantages. Each type of plan has its own restrictions, benefits, and drawbacks.

529 Education Plans

With a 529 plan, you contribute money to be used for the higher education expenses of a family member. No income tax is imposed on increases in the worth of plan funds, or on distribution of plan funds for your beneficiary's higher education expenses. A person can contribute up to $15,000 per year free from gift tax to each 529 account established. (For more information about gift taxes, see "Making Gifts During Life," in Chapter 10.)

There are two types of basic 529 plans and most 529 programs offer more than one version of each type:

- **Savings plans.** With a savings plan, you make contributions to an investment account established for a minor's education costs. The account functions much like an IRA or a 401(k) account; your money is placed in mutual funds or similar investments. You hope the value of these assets rises substantially by the time the minor starts college. Each 529 program has a state-set contribution limit—usually the approximate cost for four years of college in that state.

- **Prepaid plans.** With a prepaid plan, you pay in advance for all or part of the costs of a public college education in your state. These plans are not an investment; what you've paid into the plan is what will be available for college costs. A prepaid plan may be converted to pay for the costs of out-of-state and private colleges. "Independent" 529 plans are available as pay-in-advance plans for private colleges.

529 programs are state-run and each state sets its own rules about account management, fees, and contribution limits, and many other issues. You can join a 529 program in a state other than your state of residence; however, not all states allow nonresidents to use their 529 programs. Try comparing plans at www.savingforcollege.com.

A 529 plan is essentially a securities investment, so it comes with the stock market pitfalls we're all aware of. As the legendary Wall Street investor Bernard Baruch observed, the only thing certain about the stock market is that "prices will fluctuate." Still, 529 accounts are quite popular; they now hold many billions of dollars.

RESOURCE
Get more information about 529 plans. To read more about 529 plans, start with the United States Securities and Exchange Commission's publication *Introduction to 529 Plans,* available online at SEC.gov. And you can drill down for details by state at www.savingforcollege.com.

Coverdell Education Accounts

With a Coverdell account, you can contribute a total of $2,000 per year for a beneficiary's educational expenses. Increases in the worth of the account are tax free, and no income tax is assessed when funds are withdrawn to pay for qualified expenses.

The $2,000 limit is the total amount that can be set aside in any one year for any one beneficiary. Though this $2,000 limit restricts the appeal of a Coverdell account, the account can still be useful in the right circumstances. For example, a Coverdell account can work well for a family with young children and not much money. Each year, for each child, the parents put whatever they can afford, up to $2,000 per child, into a Coverdell account. At that rate, the total saved could be quite helpful when a child attends college, even if the money wouldn't foot the entire bill for Stanford or Princeton. Coverdell accounts can also be useful for grandparents or other relatives who want to help a child, while the parents invest in a 529 account or save in other ways to cover the costs of higher education.

ABLE Accounts for Disability Expenses

The federal Achieving a Better Life Experience Act (ABLE Act) allows states to provide 529-type accounts for people with disabilities. The key feature of these accounts is that the money saved in these accounts does not count against the account holder's eligibility for government disability benefits. So people with disabilities can save a little bit of money without jeopardizing the benefits on which many depend.

By law, all ABLE accounts come with significant limitations:

- **Qualification restrictions.** ABLE accounts are only available to people who fall under the Social Security's definition of "disabled," and the disabling condition must have started prior to reaching age 26.
- **Balance limits.** Any balance over $100,000 counts against SSI eligibility.
- **Contribution limits.** Annual contributions for each account cannot exceed the individual gift tax exclusion ($15,000 in 2020). Also, each ABLE program sets a maximum contribution—usually equal to the state's 529 account limit ($300,000–$500,000, depending on the state).

- **Medicaid payback.** If the account holder dies having received Medicaid payments, Medicaid can demand repayment from any remaining account funds.
- **Restricted use of funds.** Funds in ABLE accounts can only be used for "Qualified Disability Expenses." This is a broad category that includes expenses for housing, education, transportation, employment training, health and wellness, financial management, legal fees, and more.

Most states currently administer ABLE accounts. However, a handful are still developing their programs and a few states have opted not to offer ABLE accounts at all. You don't have to open an ABLE account in the state you live in; you can open one run by another state that has opened its program to nonresidents. Learn more about ABLE accounts and compare plans on the website of the ABLE National Resource Center, www.ablenrc.org.

Leaving Property to Adult Children

If you believe that one or more of your adult children is not capable of handling property responsibly, you can use one of several types of trusts to impose controls over his or her inheritance. Some of these trusts, such as a spendthrift trust, are complex and must be drafted by a lawyer. (See Chapter 11.) Or, you can use a child's trust to postpone the age at which your child receives property outright.

> EXAMPLE: Franklin, a single parent, creates a living trust leaving his estate, worth $340,000, equally to his two children—Todd, 25, and Carolyn, 23. Todd has always been frugal with money, if not parsimonious. He's been saving since his first allowance. Carolyn is the flip side of the coin. She runs through whatever cash she has with speed and flamboyance, and from Franklin's perspective, often moves beyond generosity with money to

recklessness. In his living trust, Franklin leaves Todd his half of the estate outright. However, he places Carolyn's half in a child's trust, with Franklin's brother Joe—a stable type if ever there was one—as trustee. Carolyn will not receive any trust property outright until she turns 35. By that age, Franklin hopes she will have become sensible enough to manage a large amount of money. In the meantime, Joe will manage the trust in Carolyn's interest.

This example is nice and simple (that's its point), but how desirable would it be in real life? Would Franklin—or you—really want to have one child's property held in trust while another child is left money outright? It's possible that such an arrangement would create emotional harm that far outweighs whatever fiscal prudence might be gained. So, once again, I stress that there are no rigid rules in estate planning. You always have to place legal options in the deeper context of human relationships.

Leaving Property to Other People's Children

If you want to leave property to minor or young adult children who aren't your own, perhaps your grandchildren or children from another family, you have the following choices:

- You can leave small gifts—roughly worth under $2,000—directly to the child, if you believe he or she will handle the property responsibly.
- For larger gifts, you can leave the gift outright to the child's parent, and rely on the parent to use the gift for the benefit of the child.
- Leave the gift under the Uniform Transfers to Minors Act, discussed above. This is best suited for gifts up to $200,000. The child must receive the gift property outright at the age set by state law—21 in the majority of states, 18 in most others, and up to 25 in a few. You leave the gift to an adult custodian you name, who manages the property until it is turned over to the child.

- Create a child's trust for the gift. You name the trustee of each child's trust, to manage all property in it. Doing this makes sense for large gifts—those above the $200,000 you might leave under the UTMA. This method often makes good sense for large gifts to grandchildren, particularly if the trustee is the child's parent. (For more information, see "Trusts for Children," above, if you're leaving property to a minor, or "Leaving Property to Adult Children," above, if you want to leave property to a young adult.)

The least desirable method is simply to leave the gift in your will without selecting a method for adult supervision. Court proceedings will be necessary to appoint a property guardian to supervise the gift. And because you are not the child's parent, you can't even appoint or suggest a property guardian for him or her in your will. ●

Planning for Incapacity: Medical Care and Finances

A s we grow older, we face the possibility of becoming mentally or physically incapacitated (or both) for some period of time, perhaps even for many years. Though it may be difficult to consider your own incapacity, wise planning means taking this bleak possibility into account. In particular, life-support issues can become confusing and contentious if you become incapacitated without a clear written statement of your desires regarding continuing treatment. You can plan ahead by preparing a few simple legal documents to ensure that your medical and financial wishes are carried out if you are unable to speak and act for yourself.

Of course, because unforeseen accidents and illnesses are possible, it's sensible to prepare these documents as part of your estate plan, no matter what your age or the state of your health. Functionally, they work as a kind of insurance, becoming operational only if you in fact become unable to manage your own affairs.

RESOURCE

Planning for long-term medical care. You may also want to plan for the possibility that you'll need long-term medical care. This is covered in *Long-Term Care: How to Plan & Pay for It,* by Joseph Matthews (Nolo).

Medical Decisions

In recent decades, the increasing use of life-sustaining medical technology has raised fears in many that our lives may be artificially prolonged against our wishes. The right to die with dignity, and without the tremendous agony and expense for both patient and family caused by prolonging lives artificially, has been confirmed by the U.S. Supreme Court, the federal government, and every state legislature.

Planning for Incapacity: Vocabulary

Several terms used in this chapter sound similar but have distinct meanings. Here's a chart to help you keep them straight.

Term	Also Called	What It Means
Living Will	• Directive to Physicians • Health Care Declaration • Medical Directive • Health Care Directive	A legal document in which you state your wishes about life support and other kinds of medical treatments. The document takes effect if you can't communicate your own health care wishes.
Durable Power of Attorney for Health Care	• Medical Power of Attorney • Power of Attorney for Health Care • Designation of Surrogate • Patient Advocate Designation	A legal document in which you give another person permission to make medical decisions for you if you are unable to make those decisions yourself.
Advance Health Care Directive		Any of the documents discussed above may be called an advance health care directive; the term most often refers to a legal document that includes both a health care declaration and a durable power of attorney for health care. This type of combined form is currently used in more than one-third of the states.
Do-Not-Resuscitate (DNR) Order	DNR Form, DNR Directive, Comfort One	A medical order or form, usually signed by a doctor, that documents your wish not to receive CPR or other invasive resuscitation techniques if you stop breathing or your heart stops beating.

Planning for Incapacity: Vocabulary (continued)

Term	Also Called	What It Means
Physician Order for Life-Sustaining Treatment (POLST)	Provider Order for Life-Sustaining Treatment, Physician Orders for Scope of Treatment (POST), Medical Orders for Scope of Treatment (MOST), Medical Orders for Life-Sustaining Treatment (MOLST), Clinician Orders for Life-Sustaining Treatment (COLST), Transportable Physician Orders for Patient Preferences (TPOPP)	A medical order signed by a doctor or other qualified health care professional. A POLST form is used in health care settings to document your instructions for medical care at the end of life. It is not a substitute for an Advance Health Care Directive.
Health Care Agent	• Attorney-in-Fact for Health Care • Patient Advocate • Health Care Proxy • Surrogate • Health Care Representative	The person you name in your durable power of attorney for health care to make medical decisions for you if you cannot make them yourself.
Durable Power of Attorney for Finances		A legal document in which you give another person authority to manage your financial affairs if you become incapacitated.
Attorney-in-Fact for Finances	Agent for Finances	The person you name in your durable power of attorney for finances to make financial decisions for you if you cannot make them yourself.
Springing Power of Attorney		A durable power of attorney that takes effect only when and if you become incapacitated.

Writing down your wishes for medical care and appointing a trusted person to be sure those wishes are carried out can help alleviate fears, whether you worry about receiving unwanted medical treatment or you want health care providers to do all they can to prolong your life. It can also be a huge help to family members who might otherwise agonize about making medical decisions on your behalf.

Living Wills and Powers of Attorney for Health Care

Every state has laws authorizing individuals to create simple documents setting out their wishes concerning life-prolonging medical care. There are two basic types of medical care documents you need to prepare to ensure you'll receive the care you want.

First, you need a "living will" or "declaration," a written statement to medical personnel that spells out the medical care you do or do not want to receive if you are incapacitated. (The term "living will" should not be confused with the conventional will you use to leave your property at death.) Your declaration functions as a contract with the treating doctor, who must either honor your wishes for medical care or transfer you to another doctor or facility that will honor them.

Second, you'll want a "durable power of attorney for health care" (sometimes called a "medical power of attorney," "designation of health care surrogate," or "patient advocate designation"). In this document you appoint someone you trust to be your health care agent (sometimes called an "attorney-in-fact for health care" or "health care proxy") to see that your doctors and other health care providers give you the kind of medical care you wish to receive. In many states, you can also give your health care agent greater authority to make decisions about your medical care, including:

- hiring and firing medical personnel
- visiting you in the hospital or other facility even when other visiting is restricted

- admitting you to a nursing home
- having access to medical records and other personal information, and
- getting court authorization if it is required to obtain or withhold medical treatment if, for any reason, a hospital or doctor does not honor your health care wishes.

Because your agent may have broad authority to direct your health care, it is crucial that you appoint someone who understands your wishes and will carry them out faithfully. Ideally, you will also name someone who:

- is likely to be present when decisions need to be made—most often, this means someone who lives nearby or who is willing to travel and spend time at your side during hospitalization
- will not easily be swayed or bullied by doctors or family members who disagree with your wishes, and
- is capable of grasping your medical condition and any proposed medical treatments.

You should not appoint your doctor as your health care agent. In fact, laws in most states specifically forbid treating physicians from acting as a patient's health care agent. This eliminates the risk that they will have their own interests at heart and fail to act purely according to your wishes.

As long as you are of sound mind, you can change your health care documents in any way you wish, including appointing a new agent.

In addition to these two documents, you may wish to create a document that describes your wishes for care in a medical emergency. (See "In an Emergency: DNR Orders and POLST Forms," below.)

What You Can Cover

As mentioned above, your living will is the place to write out what you do and do not want in terms of medical care if you are unable to speak for yourself. You don't need to become a medical expert to complete your documents, but it will help you to become familiar with the kinds of medical procedures that are commonly administered to patients who are seriously ill. These may include:

- medications to relieve pain and keep you comfortable
- artificially administered food and water (feeding tubes)
- blood and blood products
- cardiopulmonary resuscitation (CPR)
- diagnostic tests
- dialysis
- antibiotics and other drugs
- respirators, and
- surgery.

Making decisions about these kinds of medical procedures may appear straightforward at first, but preparing your documents actually involves serious, often difficult, decision making. For instance, do you want to require, allow, or discontinue artificial feeding and hydration (water) through tubes? Under what circumstances? Do you want your attorney-in-fact to be able to decide these matters?

> **CAUTION**
> **Discuss your decisions thoroughly with your health care agent.** In reality, making health care decisions for another person can be complex, even wrenching. The medical situation may be far from clear. Chances of recovery may be uncertain. The unfortunate truth is that not all possibilities can be anticipated, so precise instructions can't always be given in a durable power of attorney for health care. Your agent may be called upon to make hard choices. The more he or she understands about your wishes and desires regarding medical care, the better.

Obtaining up-to-date information of the state of relevant medical procedures can help you make choices about difficult issues. You can discuss these procedures with your doctor or a patient representative of your health insurance plan, or you can turn to other resources, such as *Quicken WillMaker & Trust* software (Nolo), for more detailed information.

When Your Health Care Documents Take Effect

Normally, your living will and health care power of attorney become effective when three things happen:

- you are diagnosed as close to death from a terminal condition or are permanently comatose—or, in a few states, if you have one of a number of other serious conditions

- you cannot communicate your own wishes for your medical care—orally, in writing, or through gestures, and

- the medical personnel attending you are notified of your written directions for your medical care.

In a few states, you have the option of making your health care documents effective immediately. You may choose this option if you are not yet fully incapacitated but illness or exhaustion are so great that you'd like your attorney-in-fact to start directing your health care according to your wishes.

In most instances, your documents become part of your medical record when you are admitted to a hospital or other care facility. But to ensure that your wishes will be followed if your need for care arises unexpectedly while you are out of your home state or country, it is best to give copies of your completed documents to several people, including your regular physician, health care agent, and another trusted friend.

Getting the Forms You Need

There are a number of ways to find the proper health care documents for your state; you don't need to consult a lawyer to obtain or prepare them. Here are some likely sources for forms and instructions:

- *Quicken WillMaker & Trust* software from Nolo (contains forms for all states except Louisiana, and thorough instructions to help you complete them)

- Californians can use *Living Wills & Powers of Attorney for California*, by Shae Irving (Nolo)
- local senior centers
- local hospitals (ask to speak with the patient representative; by law, any hospital that receives federal funds must provide patients with appropriate forms for directing health care)
- your regular physician
- your state's medical association, and
- the National Hospice and Palliative Care Organization, 703-837-1500, www.nhpco.org.

Finalizing Your Living Will and Health Care Power of Attorney

After you've created your health care documents, there are just a few steps you must take to finalize them. Every state requires that you sign your documents as a way of verifying that you understand them and that they contain your true wishes. If you are physically unable to sign them yourself, you can direct another person to sign them for you.

You must sign your documents, or have them signed for you, in the presence of witnesses or a notary public—sometimes both. (This depends on your state's law.) The purpose of this additional formality is so that there is at least one other person who can confirm that you were of sound mind and of legal age when you made the documents.

After your documents are complete, you should keep them where your attorney-in-fact can easily find them, if the need arises. Also, give copies to:

- your attorney-in-fact
- any physician with whom you consult regularly
- the office of the hospital or other care facility in which you are likely to receive treatment, and
- any other people or institutions you think it's wise to inform of your medical intentions.

In an Emergency: DNR Orders and POLST Forms

In addition to a living will and power of attorney for health care, some people may want to make a Do-Not-Resuscitate, or DNR, order. Some states are also supplementing or replacing DNR orders with a similar form, often known as a POLST form.

DNR Orders

A DNR order tells emergency medical personnel that you do not wish to be administered cardiopulmonary resuscitation (CPR). DNR orders are used both in hospitals and in situations where a person might require emergency care outside of the hospital. In some states, DNR orders go by a different name, such as "Comfort One." In other states, if you are using the document outside of a hospital or other health care facility, the document maybe simply called a "DNR form" or "DNR directive." Here, we use "DNR order" because that is the most common name for the document.

You may want to consider a DNR order if you:
- have a terminal illness
- are at significant risk for cardiac or respiratory arrest, or
- have strong feelings against the use of CPR under any circumstances.

In most states, any adult may secure a DNR order.

Because emergency response teams must act quickly in a medical crisis, they often do not have the time to determine whether you have a valid health care directive explaining treatments you want provided or withheld. If they do not know your wishes, they must provide you with all possible life-saving measures. But if emergency care providers see that you have a valid DNR order—which is often made apparent by an easily identifiable bracelet, anklet, or necklace—they will not administer CPR.

If you ask to have CPR withheld, you will not be given:
- chest compression
- electric shock treatments to the chest

- tubes placed in the airway to assist breathing
- artificial ventilation, or
- cardiac drugs.

If you want a DNR order, or if you would like to find out more about DNR orders, talk with a doctor. In most states, a doctor's signature is required to make the DNR valid—he or she will often need to obtain and complete the necessary paperwork. If the doctor does not have the form or other information you need, call the Health Department for your state and ask to speak with someone in the Division of Emergency Medical Services.

POLST Forms

Many states are starting to use a form that is similar to a DNR order, but differs in a few important ways. The form is often called Physician Orders for Life Sustaining Treatment (POLST), though many states use other terms, such as Clinician Orders for Life Sustaining Treatment (COLST) or Medical Orders for Scope of Treatment (MOST). A POLST form may be used in addition to—or instead of—a DNR order.

A POLST is often prepared to ensure that different health care facilities and service providers (including EMS personnel) understand a patient's wishes. In most states, a POLST form is printed on bright paper so it will easily stand out in a patient's medical records. To be valid, the form must be signed by a doctor or other approved health care professional.

Unlike a DNR order, a POLST form includes directions about life-sustaining measures—such as intubation, antibiotic use, and feeding tubes—in addition to CPR. The POLST form helps to ensure that medical providers will understand your wishes at a glance, but it is not a substitute for a thorough and properly prepared advance health care directive.

When you enter a hospital, hospice, or other health care facility, a member of the staff may ask whether you want to complete a POLST form. If not, you can ask for one.

Making Final Arrangements

When thinking about your estate plan, you might also consider making plans for a memorial service and for what you would like to have happen to your body after your death. Leaving these decisions up to your survivors may result in confusion and pain at a time that is likely already difficult. Also, without advance planning, funeral and related costs can be very expensive. It's a good idea to write out a statement describing your requests. In almost all cases, arrangements will be carried out as you specified. Do not include your statement about these wishes in your will. Your statement must be easily accessed at the time of your death, and your will may not be.

More and more people are reflecting on what they want to happen to their bodies when they die, and making choices that have emotional meaning for them and save their families needless expense. Broadly viewed, these are the choices:

- A traditional American funeral service, often including embalming of the body, conducted by a commercial funeral home, with subsequent cremation or burial.
- A simple funeral service, without embalming, either with the help of a funeral or memorial society or by independent arrangement.
- Cremation of the body. Ashes are generally returned to family members, who then save or scatter them.
- Donation of specific body organs to an organ bank. After donation, the rest of the body is normally returned for cremation or burial.
- Donation of the entire body to medical school. This must be arranged beforehand. Usually, after the body is used for studies, it is cremated.

RESOURCE

Learn more. To learn more about POLST forms, including information about POLST forms in your state, go to the POLST section of Nolo.com at www. nolo.com/legal-encyclopedia/physicians-orders-life-sustaining-treatment.

Letting People Know About Your Wishes

If you obtain a DNR order or make a POLST form, discuss your decision with your family or other caretaker. If you are keeping a DNR form at home, be sure that your loved ones or caretakers know where it is. Even if you are wearing identification, such as a bracelet or necklace, keep your form in an obvious place. You might consider keeping it by your bedside, on the front of your refrigerator, in your wallet or in your suitcase if you are traveling. If your form is not apparent and immediately available, or if it has been altered in any way, CPR will most likely be performed.

RESOURCE

Help with final arrangements. For information about making your final arrangements, you can contact the Funeral Consumers Alliance. Call 802-865-8300 or reach the organization online at www.funerals.org. You can use Nolo's *Quicken WillMaker & Trust* to create a final arrangements document, in addition to a will, health care documents, and a durable power of attorney for finances.

You may also want to check out *Get It Together: Organize Your Records So Your Family Won't Have To*, by Melanie Cullen and Shae Irving (Nolo). This book provides a complete system you can use to ensure your family and other loved ones will be able to understand and locate your wishes when the time comes.

Financial Decisions

A durable power of attorney for finances allows you to name someone you trust (called your attorney-in-fact or agent) to handle your finances if you can't. Every state recognizes this type of document. If you become unable to manage your finances and you haven't prepared a durable power of attorney, your spouse, closest relatives, or companion will have to ask a court for authority over at least some of your financial affairs. This procedure—called a "conservatorship proceeding" in most states—can be time-consuming and expensive. In contrast, preparing a durable power of attorney is simple and inexpensive—and if you do become incapacitated, the document will likely appear as a minor miracle to those closest to you.

Granting Authority to Your Attorney-in-Fact

Any power of attorney arrangement depends upon trust and understanding between you and the person you appoint to handle your affairs. You can help make this relationship work by putting specific instructions in your document regarding financial actions you do and do not wish the attorney-in-fact for finances to take. Your attorney-in-fact has only the financial authority you grant him or her in the document. Normally, an attorney-in-fact has authority to handle all regular financial matters, such as depositing checks and paying bills. Beyond the basics of routine financial maintenance, it's up to you to decide what you want to authorize.

Although you may want to define and limit your attorney-in-fact's authority in some matters, you can't, obviously, foresee every financial concern that might arise. So it's vital that you choose someone you trust and who has sound financial judgment to be your attorney-in-fact for finances. And though this doesn't have to be the same person you choose as attorney-in-fact for your health care directives (your health care agent), it's sensible to name the same person for both roles unless you strongly believe someone else should handle your money. If you do name different people for these two jobs, be sure they can work well together.

As with health care directives, you can change the attorney-in-fact for finances or any other provision of your durable power of attorney for finances any time, as long as you are of sound mind.

The Duties of an Attorney-in-Fact for Finances

Commonly, people give an attorney-in-fact broad power over their finances. But you can give your attorney-in-fact as much or as little power as you wish. You may want to give your attorney-in-fact authority to do some or all of the following:

- use your assets to pay your everyday expenses and those of your family
- buy, sell, maintain, pay taxes on, and mortgage real estate and other property
- collect benefits from Social Security, Medicare, or other government programs or civil or military service
- invest your money in stocks, bonds, and mutual funds
- handle transactions with banks and other financial institutions
- buy and sell insurance policies and annuities for you
- manage your digital assets
- file and pay your taxes
- operate your small business
- claim or disclaim property you inherit or are otherwise entitled to
- represent you in court or hire someone to represent you, and
- manage your retirement accounts.

Whatever powers you give the attorney-in-fact for finances, he or she must act in your best interests, keep accurate records, keep your property separate from his or hers (unless you specify otherwise in the power of attorney document), and avoid conflicts of interest.

RESOURCE

How to find the forms you need. You can use *Quicken WillMaker & Trust* (software from Nolo) to prepare a durable power of attorney for finances that is valid in your state.

When Your Durable Power of Attorney for Finances Takes Effect

There are two kinds of durable powers of attorney for finances: those that take effect immediately, and those that don't become effective unless someone certifies that you are incapacitated. Which to choose depends, in part, on when you want your attorney-in-fact for finances to begin handling tasks for you.

If you want someone to take over some or all of your financial tasks now, you should make your document effective as soon as you sign it. Then, your attorney-in-fact can begin helping you with your finances right away—and can continue to do so if you later become incapacitated.

On the other hand, you may feel strongly that your attorney-in-fact for finances should not take over unless and until you are incapacitated. In this case, you have two options. If you trust your attorney-in-fact to use his or her authority only when it's absolutely necessary, you can go ahead and make your durable power of attorney effective immediately. Legally, your attorney-in-fact for finances will then have the authority to act on your behalf—but, according to your wishes, won't do so unless he or she ever decides that you can't handle your affairs yourself.

If you're uncomfortable making a document that's effective immediately, you can make a "springing" power of attorney that doesn't take effect until a person you have named in the document declares, in writing, that you have become incapacitated and can't manage your finances.

TIP

There are extra steps if you want your doctor to determine your incapacity. Traditionally, the declaration of incapacity was made by a doctor. However, this has become problematic because federal privacy laws restrict medical professionals' ability to release patient information. If you would like your doctor to be able to make a determination about your incapacity, talk to your doctor about what releases you'll need to sign in order to authorize him or her to make a determination.

There can be inconveniences involved in creating a springing power of attorney. First, your attorney-in-fact will have to go through the potentially time-consuming and complicated process of getting the declaration of incapacity. And second, though it's not too likely, some people and institutions may be reluctant to accept a springing power of attorney, even after your attorney-in-fact has obtained the necessary statements. A bank, for example, might question whether you have, in fact, become incapacitated. These hassles could delay your attorney-in-fact and disrupt the handling of your finances.

If you truly trust your attorney-in-fact for finances (and you should), you may find that it makes more sense to create a document that's effective immediately and then make clear to your attorney-in-fact when he or she should take action under the document. Ultimately, of course, the decision is yours—and you should choose the option that feels most comfortable to you.

Finalizing Your Durable Power of Attorney for Finances

After you've completed your durable power of attorney for finances, you must observe certain formalities to make it legal. But these requirements aren't difficult to meet.

You must sign your durable power of attorney in the presence of a notary public for your state. In some states, notarization is required by law to make the durable power of attorney valid and notarization is always required to record a power over real property. (See below.) But even where law doesn't require it, custom does. A durable power of attorney that is not notarized may not be accepted by people your attorney-in-fact needs to deal with. A handful of states also require you to sign your document in front of witnesses. Witnesses must be mentally competent adults, and your attorney-in-fact may not be a witness. Some states impose additional witness requirements as well, and a few require your attorney-in-fact to sign the power of attorney or a separate consent form before taking action under the document.

Finally, if your document grants power over real estate, you must put a copy of your document on file in the land records office of any counties where you own real estate. This process is called "recording" or "registration." In South Carolina, you must record your durable power of attorney for it to be durable—that is, for it to remain in effect if you become incapacitated.

What to Do With the Signed Document

If your power of attorney is effective immediately, give the original signed and notarized document to the attorney-in-fact for finances. He or she will need it as proof of authority to act on your behalf.

If the durable power of attorney won't become effective unless you become incapacitated (a springing durable power of attorney), keep the notarized, signed original yourself. Store it in a safe, convenient place that the attorney-in-fact can reach quickly, if necessary. Your attorney-in-fact will need the original document to carry out your wishes.

You may also wish to give copies of your durable power of attorney to the people and institutions your attorney-in-fact for finances will need to deal with—banks or government offices, for example. If the document is already in their records, it may eliminate hassles for your attorney-in-fact later. If you're making a springing durable power of attorney, however, it may seem premature to contact people and institutions about a document that may never go into effect. It's up to you.

Wills

A will is what many people think of when they first consider estate planning. This makes sense. Everyone should have a will, whether or not they engage in more extensive planning. And many people decide that a will is all the planning they need, at least for the time being.

A will is simply a legal document, usually only a few pieces of paper, in which you name the people who will receive your property after you die (more accurately, all property left by the will). Normally, you name:

- direct beneficiaries, to receive specific property left to them
- alternate beneficiaries, to receive property left to any direct beneficiaries who die before you do, and
- one or more residuary beneficiaries (and alternates), to receive all property not left to other beneficiaries under your will.

A will can also serve other vital purposes, such as appointing a personal guardian to raise your young children. (See "Naming Someone to Care for Young Children," in Chapter 3.) Wills do have a few technical requirements, but not as many as you might fear; you can readily master the technicalities.

You can name whomever you want as beneficiaries of your will property. And if your situation calls for it, you can use your will to establish a child's trust, family pot trust, or custodianship under the UTMA. (See "Choosing How Your Children's Property Should Be Managed," in Chapter 3.)

Will Requirements

Although most people know what a will is, at least in a general sort of way—something to do with property after a death—I've had a number of people tell me they don't really understand what a will does, how it works, or what it requires. For example, they wonder if a will has to be typed. And isn't there something about witnesses? Must a will be notarized? Filed with some judicial agency? Prepared with a valid stamp? Must there be gobs of legalese in a will? Isn't it inherently dangerous to try to prepare a will without using a lawyer?

Here are short answers to each of these questions; I'll develop each answer later in this chapter. Yes, a will should be typed, although there are a few exceptions. Yes, you must have at least two people witness your will. No, it does not have to be notarized. No, it does not have to be filed with some judicial agency—as long as you're alive. After you die, the will must normally go through a court proceeding called probate. No stamp or other official imprimatur is required. And, no, a will doesn't have to be gorged with legalese. Finally, for most people, there is no danger in preparing a will without a lawyer.

Though there aren't many formalities necessary to prepare a valid will, you do have to be sure your will complies with what is required. The problem here is that you can't rely solely on common sense. You must know the rules.

> **EXAMPLE:** Ramona meant to prepare some kind of estate plan after her daughter, Laura, was born, six years ago. But neither she nor her partner, Ray, ever managed to get it done. Then Ramona got the chance to work at a film festival in Eastern Europe for three weeks. Only just before leaving did she handwrite a letter, stating that if she died, she wanted her property used to take care of Laura. After she'd safely returned, she asked me if this paper would work as her will. After asking her some questions, I told her that, unfortunately, it wouldn't. She had failed to meet certain mandatory requirements for a document to be a valid will.

Here are all the legal requirements for a valid will:
- You must be at least 18 years old.
- You must be "of sound mind." (The fact that you can read and understand this book is sufficient to establish that you are.)
- The document should be typed using a typewriter or computer. This is required in about half the states, and safest in all.
- The document must state that it is your will.

- You must leave some property to at least one beneficiary and/or appoint a personal guardian for any minor children.
- You must sign and date your will.
- There must be at least two witnesses who watch you sign your will and then sign it themselves. They do not have to know its contents.

EXAMPLE: To return to Ramona's letter, it failed to work as a will on several grounds. First the letter was handwritten and therefore invalid in many states. Next, the letter didn't state that it was her will. Third, she had not dated the letter. Ramona had also overlooked three vital concerns: (1) leaving her property to Laura, (2) naming Ray to manage that property until Laura becomes an adult, and (3) determining who should raise Laura if neither she nor Ray could.

While there's no requirement that a will be notarized, you may decide to use a notary when your will is signed and witnessed. In most states, having the witnesses sign a brief statement called a "self-proving" affidavit, which is then notarized, can eliminate any need for a witness to testify at subsequent probate proceedings.

A Will That Looks Like a "Real Will"

There are no appearance requirements for a will, beyond that it be legible. Physically, a will really is nothing more than some paper with typing or printing. But years ago, when I practiced law with two friends, we learned that some clients were disappointed at receiving a will that seemed so ordinary. So our flamboyant partner stapled each new will into a blue binder, closed this document with red ribbon, and then sealed it with a red wax stamp. The wills looked vaguely aristocratic—or at least medieval—some clients were happier, and we charged more.

Your Executor

When you make a will, one primary decision is appointing your "executor" —that is, the person with legal responsibility for carrying out the terms of your will. The executor (called a "personal representative" in some states) has legal authority to represent your estate, including supervising the distribution of property left by your will. Your executor may also have other tasks, ranging from locating will assets to filing estate tax returns.

An Executor's Duties

Executors can have a number of duties, depending on the complexity of the deceased person's estate. Typically, an executor must:

- Decide whether or not probate proceedings are necessary. If the will property is worth less than a certain amount, formal probate may not be required. (See "Probate," below.)
- If probate is required, file the will and all required legal papers in the local probate court.
- Manage the deceased person's property—including digital assets— during the probate process, which may take up to a year.
- Set up an estate bank account, both for paying bills and to hold money paid to the estate—for example, paychecks or stock dividends.
- Pay taxes, including a final income tax return for the deceased, and any federal or state estate tax return due.
- Supervise the distribution of the deceased's will property to the beneficiaries.

RESOURCE

Understanding the executor's job. If you want to learn more about an executor's duties, including what you can do to make your future executor's job easier, turn to *The Executor's Guide: Settling a Loved One's Estate or Trust*, by Mary Randolph (Nolo).

Your executor should be someone you fully trust who's willing to do the job. You should also name a successor executor in case, for any reason, your first choice can't serve. If you plan to prepare a living trust, it's generally best that your executor be the same person you chose to be the successor trustee of your trust. (See "How a Living Trust Works," in Chapter 6.) Also, if possible, it's best to name an executor who lives in your state, or near it. Some states impose extra requirements on out-of-state executors.

You can name coexecutors, or even several executors, if you want to. Of course, it's simpler to name just one executor, but there can be compelling reasons—family harmony is one common example—for selecting more than one. If you have more than one, you must resolve whether any one of them can act independently on behalf of your estate, or if all (or a majority) must agree before acting. The first option has obvious risks, such as two trustees taking opposing actions, while the latter option can be very clumsy in practice, generating much paperwork. At the least, if you want multiple executors, be sure they all get along very well.

Some conventional estate planners recommend selecting a bank or trust company to be your executor. I strongly recommend against this, unless you have no other alternative. First of all, most financial institutions won't take the job for a modest estate. More important, your executor is your link to the future, in charge of distributing your property after your death. You want someone human, with genuine concern, not an impersonal institution that charges fees for every small act. If your most trusted friend is your banker, name her as executor, but not the bank itself.

Types of Wills

Here I'll define some types of wills other than the basic will I described above.

Handwritten Wills

A handwritten will (called "holographic" in legalese) must be written, dated, and signed entirely in the handwriting of the person making the will. It does not have to be witnessed. Handwritten wills are recognized by about 25 states. But I definitely don't recommend them, even in the states where they're legal.

Handwritten wills aren't desirable because probate courts have traditionally been very strict when examining them after the death of the writer. Because a handwritten will isn't normally witnessed, judges sometimes fear that it might have been forged. Also, a judge may require proof that the will was actually and voluntarily written by the deceased person, which can be difficult to demonstrate. Hiring a handwriting expert isn't cheap. In short, given the tiny bit of extra trouble it takes to prepare a typed or printed will and have it witnessed, it's reckless not to do it.

Pour-Over Wills

A "pour-over" will directs that the property subject to it goes to (is "poured over" into) a trust. For example, sometimes people make their living trusts the beneficiaries of their wills. When the will property is poured over to the trust, the trust document controls who receives that property.

In my opinion, pour-over wills are normally not desirable. The purpose of a living trust is to avoid probate. (See Chapter 6.) Using a pour-over will simply ensures that some property that will eventually wind up in the trust must nevertheless go through probate. It's better to put property into the trust in the first place, when you create it.

However, a pour-over will can be helpful in a few situations. If you create a child's trust or a family pot trust in your living trust, you may want any will property to pour over to the living trust and become part of the property in the child's trust or family pot trust. (Child's trusts and family pot trusts are discussed in Chapter 3.) Otherwise, you'd have to set up two child's or family pot trusts—one in your will, another in your living trust. A pour-over will can eliminate this kind of wasteful duplication.

EXAMPLE: Ben and Mary create a shared living trust, each naming the other as primary beneficiary. Each also names their two young children as alternate beneficiaries. They create a family pot trust to hold any of the living trust property the children might inherit before the youngest turns 18.

Ben and Mary each also create wills to transfer their cars, personal checking accounts, and a few other minor items. They make their wills "pour over" to their living trusts.

Ben and Mary die in a car crash, when their children are nine and 12. All property subject to their wills is poured into the living trust. Under the provisions of the trust, that property becomes part of the family pot trust to benefit the children.

Ben and Mary created only one family pot trust, because of their pour-over wills. Otherwise, each would have had to create three pot trusts, one in each will, another for the living trust property.

Candidly, it's my impression that some lawyers push pour-over wills because they not only sound sophisticated, they ensure that at least some probate fees can be collected.

Statutory Wills

A statutory will is a preprinted, fill-in-the-blanks, check-the-boxes will form authorized by state law. California, Maine, Massachusetts, Michigan, New Mexico, and Wisconsin have statutory wills. In theory, statutory wills are an excellent idea—inexpensive, easy to complete, and reliable. Unfortunately, in practice, statutory wills are so limited in scope that they aren't useful for most people. The choices provided in the statutory forms are quite narrow and cannot legally be changed—that is, you can't customize them to fit your situation or, indeed, change them at all. For example, the Michigan form allows you to make only two cash gifts (aside from household property); everything else must go to your spouse or children.

Normally, statutory wills are useful only if you are married and want all or the bulk of your property to go to your spouse—or, if he or she predeceases you, in trust for your minor children. Because of the limitations of statutory wills, the movement to introduce them in other states has stalled.

Electronic Wills

Electronic wills are created, signed, and stored electronically. To make an electronic will, a testator writes a will on a computer, tablet, or phone, signs it electronically, has witnesses sign it, and then saves it to the device. Only three states (Arizona, Florida, Indiana, and Nevada) have passed statutes allowing electronic wills. In all other states, wills have to be signed physically on paper by the testator and the witnesses.

There may come a time when nearly all states allow electronic wills, but that time is not now. Currently, there is no consensus about some key issues. For example, does typing one's name suffice as a signature, do witnesses need to be physically present with the testator, how will the testator's identity be verified, what are the requirements for revocation, and can a will validly made in a state that allows electronic wills be probated in a state that doesn't allow them? Until these issues are settled and electronic wills are explicitly permitted in the majority of states, make your will the traditional way—typewritten on paper, signed with a pen, and in the presence of two witnesses who also sign.

Oral Wills

Oral wills (also called "nuncupative" wills) are not allowed in most states. In the few states where they are permitted, they are so restricted that they have little or no practical usage. For example, some states allow oral wills only if the will maker spoke under the perception of his imminent death on a battlefield.

Video or Film Wills

Video or film wills are not valid under any state's law.

> **SEE AN EXPERT**
> **Using video to avoid lawsuits over your will.** If you fear that someone may contest your will, ask a lawyer about using videotape or film to help establish that you were thinking clearly, and not under coercion, when your will was signed.

Probate

Unless exempt under state law, all property left by will must go through probate, a tedious and expensive court process.

Many people, including, I'm sure, many readers of this book, wisely know they want the bulk, or even all, of their property to avoid probate. Indeed, far too many people have learned, often from bitter family experience, that the lawyer-infested probate process is costly and time-consuming—and that it usually provides no benefits, except to attorneys.

Simplified Probate for Small Estates

Some states don't require probate—or they offer greatly simplified probate—for "small" or "modest" estates. Under some states' probate-exemption laws, even a "modest" estate can have a substantial amount of money. In California, for example, an estate worth up to $166,250 is exempt from normal probate. If your estate qualifies for simplified treatment, there's no need to use any probate-avoidance device—a will is all you need.

You can learn about simplified probate in your state at www.nolo.com/legal-encyclopedia/executor-probate.

Many people aren't sure what probate actually is, except that it involves lawyers, courts, and transferring property after one's death. The actual probate functions are essentially clerical and administrative. In the vast majority of probate cases, there are no conflicts, no contesting parties—none of the normal reasons for court proceedings. Likewise, probate doesn't usually call for legal research, drafting, or lawyers' adversarial skills. Instead, in the normal, uneventful probate proceeding, the executor provides a copy of the deceased person's will and other needed financial information to a lawyer, who then initiates the court proceeding. This drags on for months, or even years, as more papers are filed, notices sent out, and routine hearings held, until a judge finally allows the will property to be distributed to the beneficiaries.

People who defend the probate system (mostly lawyers, which is surely no surprise) assert that probate prevents fraud in the transfer of a deceased person's property. In addition, they claim it protects inheritors by promptly resolving creditors' claims against the estate. In truth, however, very few estates or inheritors have any need for such "benefits," because estates rarely face any claim of fraud, or complicated debt problems. But if you have an estate with serious debt problems, including tax matters, you may want to leave your property by will, so that there's a forum for resolving these claims.

Paying Bills

Even without major debt problems, almost everyone's estate will owe a few bills, ranging from credit card charges to routine household bills. If you want, in your will you can specify a source of funds to be used to pay any last bills. By contrast, many people simply decide to let their executor choose which estate money to use for paying final bills.

If you're leaving some of your property by will, it's sensible to do what you can to keep probate fees low. You cannot, unfortunately, make a legally binding contract with a lawyer to charge a low fee. Only your executor has legal authority to make a fee agreement with a probate lawyer, because the lawyer must be responsible to a living person.

In some states, probate fees are based on the value of the property subject to probate. Here you can obviously reduce the fees by reducing the probate estate's worth. In most states, however, probate fees are charged on the basis of the number of hours the probate lawyer works. Even here, if the estate is smaller, with few big-ticket items, less work should be needed and the fees should therefore be lower.

Ways to avoid probate are discussed in detail in Chapters 6 and 7.

Property Transfers in Other Western Countries

Most Western countries use the "civil law" system, which has a different base than our legal system. In these countries, including France, Spain, The Netherlands, and Norway, there is no probate. Property transfers after death are very simple. No lawyer or judge is involved unless there is a conflict. Even England, from which we took our own fussy probate system, abolished most court probate in the 1920s. Now, England is like the Continental countries, and transfers by a will are normally handled without involving lawyers and courts.

Using a Will in Your Estate Planning

Every estate plan should include a will. But how important that will is to the overall plan varies widely. Some people make a will their entire plan. For others, a will is only a small, but essential, part of it.

A Will as the Centerpiece of Your Estate Plan

Many people reasonably decide to make a will the centerpiece—or even, in some cases, the only piece—of their estate plan. They decide that, for the foreseeable future, a will accomplishes their estate planning goals, and they can sensibly postpone more complicated, and perhaps more costly, estate planning work. You may be this kind of person if:

- No matter what your age or health, you simply don't want the bother of more extensive estate planning.
- You are healthy and statistically unlikely to die for decades. If you just want to be certain your basic wishes for your property are carried out in the very unlikely event you die suddenly, a will achieves this goal with less paperwork than other methods.
- Your primary estate planning goal is to ensure that if you die, your minor children are well cared for.

A Backup Will With a Comprehensive Estate Plan

There are many reasons to prepare a thorough estate plan: to avoid probate of most or all of your property, to plan for possible incapacity, or to address any of a number of other concerns. With a thorough estate plan do you still need a will? Definitely yes. Even if you transfer every bit of your property by a living trust, you should have at least a basic will, which I call a "backup" will, as part of your estate plan for one or more of the following reasons:

To dispose of suddenly acquired property. Anyone may acquire valuable property at or shortly before death, such as a gift or inheritance, or even a lottery prize. Of course, it's sensible to promptly revise your estate plan to name a specific beneficiary to inherit this property. But what if you don't get around to it before you die? If you have a will, that property will go to your residuary beneficiary, who, by definition, takes "the rest of your property"—that is, everything that isn't left to some other beneficiary by will or other method. If you don't have a will, state law will determine who gets such property.

To dispose of property not transferred by a probate-avoidance device. If you buy property but don't get around to planning probate avoidance for it— for example, by placing it in your living trust—a will is a valuable backup device, ensuring that the property will go to your residuary beneficiary and not pass under state law. Similarly, if somehow you've failed to transfer some of your existing property to a probate-avoidance device—for example, because you didn't properly complete transfers of title—a will directs that property to your residuary beneficiary.

To name a personal guardian for your minor children. As I've already stressed, if you have minor children, you need a will to achieve the vital goal of naming a personal guardian for them. You can't use any other device for this purpose, except a living trust in a couple of states. Also, you can use your will to appoint a property guardian for your children, someone who will manage any of their property not otherwise legally supervised by an adult. All of these issues are discussed in Chapter 3.

In case probate is not required. As mentioned above, small or modest estates may be altogether exempt from probate. In some states, even larger estates can benefit from probate-exemption laws. In California for example, property transferred by probate-avoidance methods doesn't count toward the $166,250 probate-exemption limit. So even wealthy Californians can use a will for leaving lesser gifts—that treasured antique clock to a niece, $15,000 to a friend, stock worth $18,000 to a fondly remembered employee—without ensnaring that property in probate as long as the total value left by will is under $166,250. The bulk of the estate, all property worth over $166,250, is transferred by probate-avoidance methods.

To leave property you've inherited that is still in probate. On the off chance that someone leaves you property by will, and that property is still enmeshed in probate when you die, you need a will to specify who gets that property. Other transfer devices won't work.

What If You Die Without an Estate Plan?

If you die without an estate plan that instructs how to distribute your property, you have died "intestate" and the state will distribute your property for you. States use "intestate succession laws" to determine who gets what. These laws distribute property to the deceased's closest relatives following a determined scheme. Generally, property first goes to the spouse and the children of the deceased. If there is no spouse and no children, it goes to the next closest relative, usually the parents, and then to the siblings of the deceased, and so on.

EXAMPLE: Malcolm dies intestate in California. Malcolm does not have children, his wife recently died, and his parents passed long ago. Although Malcolm's brother Richard has also passed away, Richard's daughter is still living. According to California's intestate succession laws, she will acquire what's left of Malcolm's estate after a court-assigned administrator pays the estate's bills (including his substantial fees) and taxes.

To learn about intestate succession in your state, go to www.nolo.com/legal-encyclopedia/intestate-succession.

Property You Can't Transfer by Will

Now that we've seen why a will is always a good idea, let's look at what types of property *cannot* be transferred by a will. A will usually has no effect on any property transferred by a valid probate-avoidance device. In other words, once you place property in one of the following forms of ownership, you cannot also leave that property by your will (not that you'd want to).

- **Property in a living trust.** It goes to the beneficiaries named in the trust document. (See Chapter 6.)
- **Property in a pay-on-death account, such as a bank account or stocks.** The person you designate as beneficiary on the account document inherits that property. (See Chapter 7.)

- **Property transferred by a transfer-on-death registration or deed.** Some states allow you to transfer vehicles or real estate using transfer-on-death registrations or deeds. The property passes to the named beneficiary on death, without probate. (See Chapter 7.)
- **Joint tenancy property.** At your death, your share automatically goes to the surviving joint tenants (but if all joint tenants die simultaneously, you can leave your share by will). Similar rules apply for property held in tenancy by the entirety. (See Chapter 7.)
- **Life insurance proceeds payable to a named beneficiary or beneficiaries.** The proceeds go directly to the beneficiaries. (See Chapter 7.)
- **Assets remaining in individual retirement programs, including traditional and Roth IRAs, 401(k)s, and profit-sharing plans.** The balance is payable directly to the beneficiaries you name for each plan. (See Chapter 8.)

The state of Washington has passed a law called the "superwill statute" that varies some of the rules above. (Wash. Rev. Code § 11.11.020.) If you're interested, you can read more about this law in *Plan Your Estate*, by Denis Clifford (Nolo).

Preparing Your Will

As mentioned, most people can safely prepare their wills without hiring a lawyer. Let's look realistically at what's usually involved when you prepare a will. The core transaction is probably quite simple. You've decided whom you want to get the property that will be transferred by will. There's nothing very complicated about your desires. Indeed, many people can declare in a sentence or two what they want.

> EXAMPLE 1: "I want all my property to go to my husband, Arnold Kramer, or, if he dies before I do, to be divided equally among my three children."

EXAMPLE 2: "I want all property subject to my will to go to my sister Charlotte. If she dies before me, I want this property to go to her son, Bill. If he too dies before me, I want this property sold and the proceeds divided equally among the American Red Cross, the Audubon Society, CARE, and St. Stephen's College."

EXAMPLE 3: "I want half of my property to go to my husband, Bill Tarver, and the other half divided equally between my children, Christopher Reilly and Mona Reilly Jamison."

Why should turning such straightforward desires into a valid legal document be a matter for expensive estate planning experts, or any lawyer at all? It is astounding that our legal system—perhaps "lawyers' culture" is a more apt phrase—has steeped us in the belief that any action regarding your property and who gets it at your death is so complicated that you dare not proceed without paying a lawyer. It's as if you were required to see a doctor to take aspirin.

Despite the fulminations of some lawyers, writing a basic will is not akin to creating a new computer, building a house from scratch, or (the inevitable) "brain surgery." Sure, you need useful information and carefully prepared forms, but (as I hope I've driven home by now) it's easy to get these. Some readers will decide they need or want a lawyer. Fine. Still, the important thing is not to fret over the technicalities of documents like your will. Work out what you want, and then see if you really need professional help.

RESOURCE

Learn more about making your own will. Most people can make a will without the help of a lawyer. But in some circumstances, it can be wise to seek out a lawyer's expertise. You can learn about the pros and cons of making your own will in the Wills section of Nolo.com.

Challenges to Your Will

The fact that many people worry about the possibility of lawsuits over their wills demonstrates how fear-ridden estate planning has become. Fortunately, the reality is that will challenges, let alone successful ones, are rare.

The legal grounds for contesting a will are limited to extreme circumstances. Your will can be invalidated only if:

- You were underage when you made it.
- You were clearly mentally incompetent (not of "sound mind").
- The will was procured by fraud, duress, or undue influence.
- The will does not comply with formal legal requirements (for example, only one witness was used, instead of the required two).

Substantive challenges to a will on grounds of unsound mind or fraud or duress or undue influence are difficult to prove. The courts presume that the will maker was of sound mind; a challenger must prove incapacity. Similarly, to establish fraud, duress, or undue influence, someone must prove that an evildoer manipulated the will maker, who was in a confused or weakened mental or emotional state, so that the will maker left property in a way that she or he otherwise wouldn't have.

SEE AN EXPERT

If you fear a lawsuit. If you think someone might contest your will, it's best to see a lawyer who can help you prepare in advance how to prevail against a lawsuit. It's also prudent to see an attorney if there are special circumstances that might raise questions about your competence, such as a seriously debilitating illness. This may mean having the lawyer come to see and perhaps even physically help you. For example, in many states, if you're too ill to sign your own name, you can direct that a witness or an attorney sign it for you. If someone later claims that because you were too ill to sign your name, you weren't mentally competent to make your will, the lawyer's testimony that you appeared to be in full possession of your faculties could be very important.

Living Trusts

A living trust allows you to do the same basic job as a will—that is, leave your property to the beneficiaries you choose—with the major plus of avoiding probate. Formally, a living trust is a legal document (normally, just a few pieces of paper) that controls the transfer of property in the trust after you die. In the trust document, you name beneficiaries to receive the trust property. As with a will, you name primary beneficiaries for specific property, residuary beneficiaries, and alternates for both.

Living trusts are the most popular method for transferring property without probate. They are very flexible. You can transfer all your property by living trust, or if appropriate, use one to transfer only some assets, leaving the rest by other methods.

Another plus is that living trusts are rarely made public after the trust maker's death. Wills, on the other hand, become part of the public record during the probate process.

Living trusts are called "living" because they're created while you are alive; you legally transfer property to the trust when you create it. And they're called "revocable" because you can revoke or change them at any time and for any reason before you die. While you live, you still effectively own all property you've transferred to your living trust and can do what you want with that property, including selling it, spending it, or giving it away. And don't let the word "trust" scare you. We're not talking about some monstrous monopolistic tool but a simple device that millions of savvy Americans have successfully used.

Aside from some paperwork necessary to establish a living trust and transfer property to it, there are no serious drawbacks or risks involved in creating or maintaining it. Unlike other trusts, you don't need to obtain a taxpayer ID number for the trust or maintain separate trust tax records.

All transactions that are technically made by the living trust are reported on your personal income tax return.

A living trust can work as effectively for a couple as for a single person. With a couple, each member can create his or her own separate trust. More commonly, though, a couple creates one shared living trust to handle both their shared ownership property and any property either owns individually. Because most couples who use living trusts are married, the discussion that follows uses the terms "spouses" and "marital property." However, the concepts discussed apply equally to unmarried couples.

How a Living Trust Works

Here are the basics of how a living trust works. In the trust document, you name:

- the property in the trust
- the trustee, who has authority to manage the trust property (you name yourself as the initial trustee; if you establish a shared trust, you and your spouse are the initial trustees)
- the successor trustee, who will distribute the trust property when you die
- the trust beneficiaries, who will receive the property you've left them when you die, and
- other terms of the trust, including the fact that you can amend or revoke it at any time.

Then you formally transfer property into the trust. When you die, your successor trustee simply obtains the property and transfers it to your beneficiaries. No probate or other court proceeding is required.

Living Trust Terms

The person who sets up a living trust (that's you) is called the "grantor," "trustor," or "settlor." If you establish a shared living trust with your spouse, you are both grantors. The grantor creates a written "trust document" (or "instrument"), containing all the terms and provisions of the trust.

The property you transfer to the trustee, acting for the trust, is called, collectively, the "trust property," "trust principal," or "trust estate." (And, of course, there's a Latin version: the trust "corpus," meaning the "body" of the trust.)

To place some types of property in your trust, you must formally transfer the property's title to the trust—technically, into the name of the trustee. (See "Transferring Property Into Your Trust," below.) If the trust does not become the official legal owner of property, that property is never validly included in the trust, and so can't be transferred from it when you die. Instead, that property will go to the residuary beneficiary of your will, or if you don't have a will, it will pass to a family member according to the intestacy laws of your state. In either case, it will go through probate.

With any property having a document of title, such as a house, you must prepare a new ownership document—with a house, this means making a new deed. For example, to transfer my house into my living trust, I would prepare a deed, stating that I personally transferred the house to "Denis Clifford, as trustee of the Denis Clifford Living Trust." I must then file the real estate deed with the county recorder's office— or whatever the official land records office is called in your state.

Some types of valuable property, including jewelry or art, as well as items such as household possessions or clothes, don't normally have documents of title. In that case, the property is transferred to the living trust simply by listing it in the trust document and stating that the property is owned by the trust.

The magic of the living trust is that, although it is really only a legal fiction during your life, it assumes a very real presence for a brief period after your death. When you die, your living trust can no longer be revoked or altered. Because property held in a living trust does not need to go through probate, the successor trustee can promptly transfer that property to the trust beneficiaries.

After your death, your successor trustee will need to complete some paperwork to finalize the transfers, such as new real estate deeds or other documents required by state law. The successor trustee will probably need to hire a lawyer to prepare those documents. Additionally, the successor trustee may need to:

- Obtain a written statement of the market value of trust real estate as of the date of death of the grantor. Trust real estate receives a "stepped-up basis" to its market value as of the date of the grantor's death. (See "The Federal Income Tax Basis of Inherited Property" in Chapter 9.)
- Provide essential trust information to all trust beneficiaries. Many states have specific requirements about what information must be included—another reason a lawyer may be necessary.

After the successor trustee has met all legal requirements and has distributed the property to the beneficiaries, the trust ends. No formal document of termination needs to be filed with a court or recorded.

> **EXAMPLE:** Travis wants to leave his valuable sculpture collection and his house to his daughter, Bianca, but he wants to keep complete control over the house and the collection until he dies. He also doesn't want the $500,000 value of the house and the $250,000 value of the collection to be subject to probate. Travis reasons that it's pretty silly to pay thousands of dollars in probate fees just to have his own house and sculpture turned over to his daughter after he dies.

Travis establishes a living trust, with the house and sculpture as the trust's assets. He names himself as the initial trustee. Bianca is named as both the successor trustee and the trust beneficiary. Travis prepares and records a deed that transfers the house from himself as an individual to himself as trustee of his trust. The sculpture has no documents of title, so it is effectively transferred to the trust by simply listing it as an asset in the trust document.

When Travis dies, Bianca takes possession of the sculpture. As trustee, she prepares and records a deed transferring the house from the trust— technically, from herself, as successor trustee of the trust—to herself, personally. The trust then ceases to exist.

Preparing your living trust documents is discussed in more detail, below.

Do You Need a Living Trust?

Most people who plan their estates eventually turn to a living trust to transfer some, and often the bulk, of their property. Still, not everyone needs one. Before getting deeper into a discussion of the particulars of living trusts, let's look at whether you really need one, at least for the time being. You may not want a living trust if:

You are young and healthy. The primary estate planning goals of most people in their 30s and 40s are that (1) their property be distributed as they want in the highly unlikely event they die suddenly, and (2) that any young children are cared for. A will, perhaps coupled with life insurance, generally achieves these goals more easily than does a living trust. Many younger people decide to make a will now and prepare a living trust later in life when the likelihood of imminent death is greater.

You can more sensibly transfer assets by other probate-avoidance devices. Living trusts aren't the only game in town: Pay-on-death bank or stock accounts, transfer-on-death deeds and registrations, joint tenancy, and life insurance are among the other methods that might work better for you, at least for some of your property. (See Chapter 7.)

Living Trust Seminars

Be wary of free seminars on living trusts. Usually, these events are nothing more than elaborate pitches for paying a lawyer (or some nonlawyer entity or service) $1,000 or more to prepare a living trust. Sometimes salespeople contact prospective customers by phone and pressure them to make an appointment to buy a living trust. Is it worth it? Almost always, no.

Seminar sponsors often try to sell the idea that much of your estate is likely to be gobbled up by estate tax and probate unless you set up trusts now to avoid some of the tax and buy life insurance to pay the rest. In truth, very few people have estates large enough to owe estate tax. (See Chapter 9.) Further, there are many ways to avoid probate, and you should evaluate them all before deciding what's best for you.

The sponsors won't tell you this, but instead hustle:

- lots of life insurance, to pay for supposed estate tax, and
- a fill-in-the-blanks trust that they claim will avoid probate while reducing estate tax—a version of what I call a disclaimer trust (see Chapter 10), and sometimes, an expensive annuity designed to offer financial protection in your old age.

Be sure you need these alleged benefits before paying a substantial amount for them. Do you really want to bother with probate avoidance now? If so, can you prepare your living trust yourself? Is your estate really likely to be liable for estate tax? In general, you have alternatives that are likely to work better, and cost less, than buying a living trust from a seminar.

You have, or may have, complex debt problems. If you have many creditors when you die, probate provides an absolute cut-off time for creditors to file claims against your estate. If, after being notified, they don't do so in the time permitted, your will beneficiaries can take your property free of concern that these creditors will surface later and claim a share. A living trust doesn't create any such cut-off period.

There's no one you trust to oversee your trust after your death. You need someone you fully trust to serve as successor trustee for your living trust. No court or government agency makes sure your successor trustee complies with the terms of your living trust. If you can't name a spouse, child, other relative, friend, or someone else you believe is truly trustworthy, a living trust isn't for you.

You own little property. If your property isn't worth much, monetarily speaking, probate will be unnecessary or relatively inexpensive. There isn't much point in bothering with a living trust and probate avoidance.

For all this, the fact remains that most people who plan their estates are older and are concerned with probate avoidance. For them, a living trust usually works just fine. I'm a big fan of living trusts, having seen them help many inheritors—family, friends, and clients—to receive inherited property promptly and without cost.

Living Trusts and Taxes

A probate-avoidance living trust has no effect on your taxes, either your income taxes while you live or estate tax when you die. (See Chapter 9 for a discussion of estate tax; almost all estates are not liable for any federal estate tax.) If you're looking for ways to avoid or lower taxes, or protect your assets from creditors, you are looking for something different than a living trust.

Income Tax

During your life, your living trust doesn't have a separate existence for income tax purposes. The IRS treats living trust property as it does any other property you own. Because the trust isn't functionally distinct from you while you are alive, it can't be used to lower your income tax.

Putting Your Home in a Trust: Tax Breaks

Many people put their homes—their most expensive asset—into their living trusts. If you do, you won't lose any tax benefits:

- You can still deduct mortgage interest.
- You can sell your principal home once every two years and exclude $250,000 of capital gains from income taxation. A couple can exclude $500,000.

Estate Tax

Let me state this in bold letters: **Living trusts don't save on estate tax.** I emphasize this because when some people hear the word "trust," they feel it must mean "tax savings" (or "tax scam"). To be crystal clear: All property that passes through a living trust is subject to estate tax. By itself, a living trust is designed to avoid probate, and that's all. Which is plenty.

Living Trusts and Young Children

You can leave property to minors using a living trust. For instance, many married people name their spouse as beneficiary of their trust, and their minor children as alternate beneficiaries. If you leave property in your trust to minors as direct, alternate, or residuary beneficiaries, you should use the trust document to impose adult management of that property. You accomplish this by creating a child's trust, family pot trust, or by leaving a gift using your state's UTMA. (Methods for leaving property to young children are discussed in detail in Chapter 3.)

Shared Living Trusts for Couples

The fact that a couple can create a shared living trust covering the property of both doesn't mean they must. In some circumstances, it may make sense for each spouse to create an individual living trust. For example, if each spouse owns mostly separate property, a combined living trust may make little sense. But if spouses share ownership of much or all of their property, as is often the case, it's generally preferable to use just one living trust for their property.

If you live in a community property state, in which spouses equally own most property acquired after marriage, you and your spouse almost certainly own property together. (To remind you, community property states are Arizona, California, Idaho, Louisiana, New Mexico, Nevada, Texas, Washington, and Wisconsin.)

Even in the other (common law) states, where one spouse may technically be the sole legal owner of much property, spouses who have been married for many years typically regard most or all property as owned by both. If so, you can transfer that property into legal co-ownership when creating your shared living trust.

Unmarried couples can also share ownership of property, if they choose, and register any ownership/title document in both their names as co-owners.

Setting up two separate living trusts for shared property owned by a couple is generally undesirable because ownership of the shared property must then be divided into two separate halves. That's a lot of trouble, and can cause ongoing record-keeping burdens. Worse, it can lead to unfair and undesired imbalances—for example, one spouse's stocks might go up in value while the other's decline. Fortunately, there is no need for spouses to divide property this way. With a shared trust, you can transfer all co-owned property to it. You can also put individually owned or separate property into the trust, and keep it separate. Each spouse has full power to name beneficiaries for his or her portion of the shared trust property and for all of his or her separate property.

How a Shared Living Trust Works

1. Husband and wife transfer property to trust.

2. Husband dies.

3. Trust property is divided:
    *   Husband's property—both his separate property and his portion of shared property—goes to his beneficiaries. He leaves 75% to his wife and 25% to other beneficiaries.
    *   Wife's separate property, her portion of shared property, and all property left to her by her husband is transferred to her individual revocable living trust.

4. Wife's property remains in her ongoing living trust.

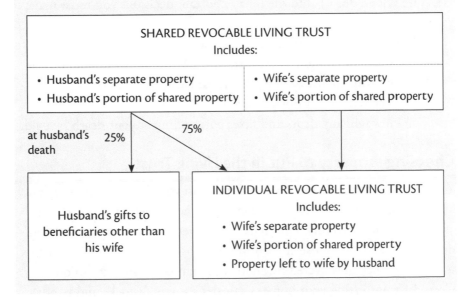

When one spouse dies, the shared living trust splits into two trusts. One trust contains all property of the deceased spouse. The other contains all property of the surviving spouse. The deceased spouse's property is transferred by the successor trustee to the beneficiaries named by that spouse. Commonly, the surviving spouse is a beneficiary, but children, friends, and organizations may also inherit property. The diagram above shows how a shared living trust works. In this example, the husband and wife transfer their property, all shared ownership, into the trust. The husband is the first spouse to die, the "deceased spouse." The wife is the "surviving spouse."

Making Key Decisions About Your Living Trust

Here, we'll look deeper into the four important decisions you must make if you want to create a living trust:

1. What property will be in the trust?
2. Who will be the successor trustee? (As I've stressed, you, or you and your spouse, will be the initial trustee(s).)
3. Who will be your beneficiaries?
4. How will any debts and taxes outstanding at your death be paid?

Choosing Property to Put in the Living Trust

You can place any amount of your property in your living trust. You can also use a living trust in combination with other transfer methods, such as pay-on-death accounts, joint tenancy, or even a will. In general, if you decide to use a living trust, it's sensible to transfer all your big-ticket items to it, unless they are covered by another probate-avoidance technique. Consider transferring your home, securities accounts (stocks and bonds), investment property, and other valuable items such as jewelry or art works.

A couple of special concerns may arise when real estate is involved:

Property taxes. In some states, transferring real estate to a new owner can result in an immediate reappraisal of the property for property tax purposes. By contrast, if the property is not transferred to new owners, it usually won't be reappraised for a set period of years, or (in a few states) at all. Because you and your living trust are considered the same basic entity while you're alive, there's no real change in ownership and therefore no reappraisal. To be absolutely sure that this is true in your state and county, check with your local property tax collector.

Homestead protection. State homestead protections, which typically protect your home equity interest from creditors up to a specific dollar amount, should not be lost because real estate is transferred to a living trust. If you are not seriously in debt, there is no need to worry about this one. However, if you're in debt and concerned that a creditor may try to force a sale of your house, check your state's homestead rules carefully.

You can also use a trust to transfer items of lesser (or no) value. A trust can be particularly useful for transferring clothes, photographs, family records, household furnishings, sports equipment, or similar possessions.

There are a couple of types of property that you generally won't want to transfer by living trust: vehicles and personal checking accounts. Living with these items while they are owned by the trust can be problematic. For example, some insurance companies may be unwilling to insure a vehicle owned by a trust rather than a person. Also, if you transfer your personal checking account into the trust, then the trust's name will be on your checks—this may not be optimal for you, and could be of concern to those receiving the check if they are unfamiliar with living trusts.

Choosing the Trustees of Your Living Trust

You must make two choices when it comes to naming a trustee to manage the property in your living trust: who will be the initial trustee, and who will take over as the successor trustee when the first trustee dies or becomes incapacitated.

Your Initial Trustee

Almost without exception, you, or you and your spouse, will be the initial trustee(s) of your living trust. If you set up a shared trust, when one spouse dies, the other continues as sole trustee. Serving as trustee is how you continue to have absolute control of your trust property.

You are not legally required to be the trustee of your trust. Occasionally, people consider naming someone else to serve as initial trustee because they don't want to, or cannot, continue to manage their own assets. But having someone else serve as sole initial trustee makes managing your living trust more complicated. Under IRS rules, separate trust records must be maintained, and a trust tax return must be filed if you aren't a trustee of your living trust.

 SEE AN EXPERT

Naming someone else as sole initial trustee. If you want to name someone besides yourself to be your initial trustee, see a lawyer. You'll probably need much more detailed controls on the trustee's powers.

Naming Cotrustees

If you want, you can name two people (or even more) to serve as initial trustees. You might do this if you want or need someone else to manage the trust property for you while you live but you don't want the IRS complications that come with an independent trustee. You name yourself and someone else as trustees and authorize either to act for the trust. Because you are, legally, one of the trustees, the IRS does not require you to keep separate trust records or file a trust tax return.

> **CAUTION**
>
> **Risks of naming a cotrustee.** If you authorize someone else to serve as a cotrustee of your trust while you are alive, that person has legal power over your trust property. Clearly this entails at least theoretical risks. The cotrustee could use some of that property for personal use, or even abscond with all of it. When you're setting up your trust, you'll need to assess whether this is an actual risk in your situation—if so, don't name a cotrustee.

Your Successor Trustee

You must name at least one successor trustee for your living trust. Your successor trustee is the person who makes your trust work after you die. With a shared trust, the successor trustee takes over after both spouses die. Also, the successor trustee is normally authorized to take over management of the trust if you (or you and your spouse, with a shared marital trust) become unable to handle it on your own.

You should also name an alternate successor trustee, in case the successor trustee dies before you do or for any other reason can't serve.

The Job of the Successor Trustee

The primary job of the successor trustee is to turn trust property over to the beneficiaries you've named in your trust. Because no court approval is required, this task is normally not difficult—as long as the property and beneficiaries are clearly identified in the trust document. Still, some effort is required. The successor trustee must know where the trust property is located. For any property held by an institution, such as banks or stock brokerage companies, the trustee must get the cooperation of the institution to turn over that property to the beneficiaries. Institutions that deal with financial assets are familiar with living trusts and how they work. They should not balk at accepting the authority of the successor trustee.

The successor trustee also prepares any new documents of title necessary to turn trust property over to the beneficiaries. The successor trustee may need to work with a lawyer to prepare the new documents of title.

In addition to dealing with property subject to formal ownership (title) documents, the trustee supervises the distribution of all other trust assets— household furnishings, jewelry, heirlooms, collectibles—to the appropriate beneficiaries. The trust ends when all beneficiaries have actually received the trust property left to them in the trust document. No document need be prepared, let alone filed with a government office, when a living trust ends. When it's work is done, it simply vanishes.

Choosing Your Successor Trustee

Your successor trustee must be trustworthy, and willing and able to do the job. Normally, this is the same person you choose as the executor of your will. (See "Your Executor," in Chapter 5.) Similarly, your alternate successor trustee is normally the person you choose for your alternate executor.

Often a principal beneficiary, such as a spouse or adult child, is named as successor trustee. However, if you believe the beneficiary (much as you love him or her) will be troubled by the practical details and paperwork, it's better to name someone else.

You can name successor cotrustees. Indeed, you can name as many successor trustees as you want, with power divided between them as you specify. However, because of problems coordinating trust management tasks and possible conflicts, it's usually risky to name multiple trustees. However, on occasion, there are compelling reasons to do so.

For example, you might name two or more children as successor cotrustees, to avoid being seen as favoring one child over others. If you name cosuccessor trustees, you need to define in the trust document how they work together. (Can any cotrustee act for the trust, or must all cotrustees agree on any decision or action taken for the trust? If all the successor trustees must agree, must agreement be in writing?) Be sure all successor cotrustees get along well. If there's any risk of conflict, naming successor cotrustees is a bad idea.

Finally, while it's possible to name a bank or trust company as successor trustee, it is usually far better to name a trusted person. Institutional trustees charge hefty fees and are more likely to be impersonal and indifferent to the needs of the beneficiaries. Additionally, many institutions will serve as trustee only for large trusts. However, naming a bank or trust company as successor trustee can make sense if you have no other options or if your family would benefit from an having impartial outsider making decisions about trust property.

Naming Your Trust Beneficiaries

You can leave each beneficiary whatever trust property you want, with one big exception. In common law states a married person may be required to leave a certain percentage of the trust estate—usually one-half—to the other spouse. However, in some common law states, the spousal-inheritance protection laws apply only to property left by will, not by living trust. Also, in almost all common law states a spouse can waive his or her spousal-inheritance rights.

> **SEE AN EXPERT**
> **See a lawyer to leave your spouse less than half of your trust property.**
> If you live in a common law state and you want to leave your spouse less than half of your trust property, see a lawyer to make sure you don't run afoul of your state's spousal-inheritance protection law.

Aside from any applicable spousal-inheritance protection law, with a shared trust you and your spouse can each choose your own trust beneficiaries. You may want to name your spouse as your sole primary beneficiary. Or you may want to divide your gifts between several people or institutions.

EXAMPLE: Malcolm and Ursula, married for 30 years, create a shared living trust. They have one child, Suzanne. Each spouse leaves the bulk of his or her property to the other. Each also leaves some smaller gifts to different relatives, friends, and charities. Both name Suzanne as their alternate beneficiary and trust residuary beneficiary. Ursula names Suzanne's husband, Tom, as her alternate residuary beneficiary. Malcolm names his niece Martha as his alternate residuary beneficiary.

Living Trusts and Your Debts

Property in a revocable living trust is not immune from attack by your creditors while you're alive. You have complete and exclusive power over the trust property, so a judge is not going to let you use the living trust (which you can revoke at any time) to evade creditors. On the other hand, if you place property in a trust that you can't revoke or change (called an "irrevocable trust"), it's a different legal matter. Your creditors cannot reach property owned by a bona fide irrevocable trust. The key words here are "bona fide." If an irrevocable trust is set up only to defraud creditors, it won't work.

Some "authorities" have inaccurately stated that property in a revocable living trust can't be grabbed by your creditors during your life. They argue that, for collection purposes, a revocable living trust is legally distinct from its creator. I know of no law or case that supports this position.

SEE AN EXPERT

Shielding your assets. If you're concerned about protecting your assets from creditors, see a lawyer.

Arranging for Payment of Debts and Taxes

Many people don't leave any substantial debt or tax obligations when they die. (Leaving a house with a mortgage isn't a concern here: The mortgage simply passes with the house.) If you have only routine bills at your death, your successor trustee and executor will pay them, either from property you earmarked in your trust or will for this purpose, or from trust or will property generally. Either way, no beneficiary will suffer a substantial loss. If you fit into this category, you can go on to other concerns. If, however, you transfer the bulk of your property by living trust and will likely have significant debts, it's best to identify trust assets that should be used to pay off these obligations. First, of course, you'll need to make a realistic appraisal (or at least a decent guess) of what you'll owe, for both regular debts and taxes, at your death.

Preparing Your Living Trust Documents

Now we'll take a closer look at preparing a living trust.

The Trust Document

No law specifies the form a living trust must take. As a result, there is no such thing as a standard living trust. Indeed, there is a bewildering variety of living trust forms, including some attorney-created forms that contain vast piles of verbiage that serve little real-world purpose, except to generate attorneys' fees.

Most likely, you'll want something simple. Aside from naming your trustee, successor trustee, and beneficiaries, your trust document contains all other provisions governing the trust. This includes identifying the trust property, usually by listing the property on one or more schedules. (In this context, a "schedule" is just a list of property attached to the main trust document.) You need only identify each item of property with sufficient clarity so that your successor trustee and beneficiaries unambiguously know what you meant. No legal rules require property to be listed in any particular form. For example, you can list property generally as "all my ballroom gowns," or "all household possessions at … (address)," or "all my books."

You must sign and date the trust document and have it notarized. Unlike wills, no witnesses are required.

Transferring Property Into Your Trust

For purposes of transferring title into the trust, there are two types of property: property that has ownership (title) documents and property that doesn't.

Property Without Ownership Documents

Many types of property don't have title documents, including all kinds of household possessions and furnishings, clothing, jewelry, furs, tools, most farm equipment, antiques, electronic and computer equipment, art works, bearer bonds, cash, precious metals, and collectibles. You transfer these items to your trust simply by listing them on a trust schedule. In addition, you can use a "notice of assignment" form, a simple document that states that the property listed on it has been transferred to the trustee's name.

Property With Ownership Documents

To make your trust effective, it is absolutely essential that you transfer ownership of property with documents of title into your trust—technically, to yourself as trustee. If you fail to do this properly, your successor trustee won't be able to transfer that property to your beneficiaries.

Property with title documents includes:
- real estate, including condominiums and cooperatives
- bank accounts
- stocks and stock accounts

- most bonds, including U.S. government securities
- corporations, limited partnerships, and partnerships
- money market accounts
- mutual funds
- safe deposit boxes, and
- vehicles, including cars, most boats, motor homes, and planes.

On the new documents of title, you formally list the trustee of the trust as the new owner. For example, if Ellen Yurok wants to place her stock account into her trust, she prepares a transfer form, listing herself (individually) as the person transferring ownership, and the new owner as "Ellen Yurok, as trustee for the Ellen Yurok Trust." (After the trust name, many lawyers add "u/t/d/" or "under trust dated" and then list the date the trust was signed and notarized.) With a shared trust, both people's names are used. Thus, Helen and Marshall Fink transfer a home from themselves to "Helen and Marshall Fink, as trustees of the Helen and Marshall Fink Trust."

Some Property Doesn't Need to Be Transferred

If you name your living trust as the beneficiary for some property, then you do not need to transfer that property into the trust. For example, if you want the proceeds of your life insurance to become part of your living trust when you die (so that it can be put into a family pot trust, for example), you don't need to transfer the policy into the trust. Rather you name the trust as the beneficiary of the insurance policy and the policy remains owned by you as an individual.

You then must file title documents, as is necessary for that type of property. With a real estate deed, you file and record it with your local land records office. With a stock market account, you give the new account form to the brokerage company. With a boat registered with the Coast Guard, you complete the appropriate Coast Guard forms (they have them) and file them with that agency.

Many estate planning lawyers insist on preparing and recording all documents transferring title to trust assets. Generally, they don't necessarily do it to raise their fees (though that is one result) but because they believe that clients can't be relied on to do the job right. I think that with clear instructional materials you can do this work yourself. But even if you end up letting a lawyer do the transfer work, you'll benefit from understanding the basic process.

You Still Need a Backup Will

Even if you decide to put everything you currently own into your living trust, you still need a backup will. This is especially true for parents of young children who will use their will to name a guardian for their kids. But all living trust makers should have a backup will to name an executor and to take care of any property that they acquire after making (and before revising) their trust. If you don't have one, you won't get to decide who gets property that passes outside of your trust. (For a full discussion about why you need a backup will, see "A Backup Will With a Comprehensive Estate Plan," in Chapter 5.)

7

Other Ways to Avoid Probate

Aside from a living trust, there are a number of other ways to avoid probate. You can mix and match these methods, using the ones that work best for you.

You might wonder why you should bother with anything but a living trust, when it seems to work so well. The answer is that in certain situations other methods are easier to use, while providing the same probate-avoidance benefits. For example, a simple pay-on-death bank account is usually a better way to handle your checking account than a living trust.

In this chapter, we'll look beyond the living trust to other probate-avoidance methods, except for using an individual retirement plan for probate avoidance, which is covered in Chapter 8.

Pay-on-Death Bank Accounts

Setting up a pay-on-death bank account—sometimes called an informal bank account trust, revocable trust account, or Totten trust—is an easy way to transfer cash at your death, quickly and without probate. All you do is designate on a form provided by the bank one or more persons you want to receive all money remaining in the account when you die.

You can do this for any kind of bank account—including savings, checking, or certificate of deposit accounts. And banks don't charge more for keeping your money this way. When you die, the beneficiary claims the money simply by showing the bank the death certificate and personal identification.

> **EXAMPLE:** Thérèse opens a savings account in her name and names Lynn Zelly as the pay-on-death (P.O.D.) beneficiary. When Thérèse dies, any money in the account will go directly to Lynn.

There are no risks in creating a P.O.D. bank account. During your life, the beneficiary has absolutely no right to the money in the account. You can withdraw some or all of the money, close the account, or change the beneficiary at any time.

Like other bank accounts, a P.O.D. account may be temporarily frozen at your death if your state levies estate tax. The state will release the money to your beneficiaries when shown that your estate has sufficient funds to pay the taxes.

Before you open a P.O.D. account, ask your bank if there are any special state law requirements about notifying the beneficiary. In a few states, a P.O.D. provision isn't effective unless you have notified the beneficiary that you've set up the account. Your bank should be able to fill you in on your state's rules. In any case, it's a good idea to tell the beneficiary you've set up the account. That way, he or she will know to take control of the account after your death.

You can also register ownership of certain kinds of government financial obligations, such as bonds, Treasury bills, and Treasury notes, in a P.O.D. form. However, you can name only one beneficiary for these securities.

Transfer-on-Death Accounts for Securities

In every state except Texas, you can add a transfer-on-death designation to individual securities (stocks and bonds) or securities accounts under the Uniform Transfer-on-Death Security Registration Act. Security accounts are broker-held accounts for your stocks, bonds, mutual funds, or similar investments.

The beneficiary or beneficiaries you designate will receive these securities promptly after your death. No probate is necessary.

Your broker should have a form that allows you to use transfer-on-death registration for a securities account. For individual stock or bond certificates, contact the company's transfer agent.

⚠️ **CAUTION**

Your broker isn't required to cooperate. Although most stockbrokers and corporate transfer agents offer transfer-on-death registration when legally permitted, the law doesn't require them to do so; it simply allows them that option. Of course, if they don't offer you the opportunity, you can threaten to switch brokers, or sell your shares, which may well overcome resistance.

Transfer-on-Death Car Registration

Some states allow vehicles to be registered in a transfer-on-death form: Arizona, Arkansas, California, Colorado, Connecticut, Delaware, Illinois, Indiana, Kansas, Maryland, Minnesota, Missouri, Nebraska, Nevada, Ohio, Oklahoma, Texas, Vermont, and Virginia. If you live in one of these states and want to use transfer-on-death registration for your vehicles, contact your state's motor vehicle agency for the appropriate form.

Avoiding Probate for Boats

In some states, such as California, transfer-on-death registration is available for small boats, called "undocumented vessels," which include the myriad of small pleasure boats that aren't required to have a valid marine document from the U.S. Bureau of Customs. In California, only one owner and one beneficiary may be listed (Cal. Veh. Code § 9852.7).

Transfer-on-Death Deeds for Real Estate

In some states, you can prepare and record a deed now that takes effect to transfer that real estate only when you die. The states that allow transfer-on-death real estate deeds are Alaska, Arizona, Arkansas, California,

Colorado, District of Columbia, Hawaii, Illinois, Indiana, Kansas, Maine, Minnesota, Missouri, Montana, Nebraska, Nevada, New Mexico, North Dakota, Ohio, Oklahoma, Oregon, South Dakota, Texas, Utah, Virginia, Washington, West Virginia, Wisconsin, and Wyoming. You can revoke a transfer-on-death deed at any time before your death.

The deed should expressly state that it does not take effect until your death and name the person(s) to receive title to the real estate after your death. A transfer-on-death deed must be drafted, signed, notarized, and recorded (filed in the county land records office) just like a regular deed. In Ohio, you must use a specific form called a "Transfer on Death Affidavit."

RESOURCE

Get a state-specific transfer-on-death deed from Nolo. Nolo provides transfer-on-death deeds for many states that allow them. The forms come with clear, plain-English instructions on how to use them. Go to www.nolo.com and search for "transfer-on-death deed."

CAUTION

Don't try this unless you know your state law authorizes it. You cannot use a deed to transfer real estate at your death unless your state law (or the state law where the real estate is located) specifically allows it.

Joint Tenancy

In the right circumstances, joint tenancy can be a very handy probate-avoidance device. The key to deciding whether you want to use it for some of your property is to see if your needs fit within those circumstances.

How Joint Tenancy Works

Joint tenancy is a form of shared property ownership. For estate planning purposes, the most important characteristic of joint tenancy is that when one owner (called a joint tenant) dies, the surviving joint owner or owners automatically inherit the deceased owner's share. This is called the "right of survivorship." The property doesn't go through probate. There is some simple paperwork that must be completed to transfer the property into the name of the surviving owner(s), but this can be easily done.

> EXAMPLE: Evelyn and Joe own a house in joint tenancy. Evelyn dies. Because Joe has the "right of survivorship," he inherits Evelyn's share of the house, without probate. Joe is now the sole owner of the house.

By contrast, other forms of shared ownership, such as "tenancy in common," or corporate or partnership interests, do not create a right of survivorship.

Joint tenancy is most commonly used for real estate, though it is legally available for all types of property.

A joint tenant cannot leave his or her share to anyone other than the surviving joint tenants. So even if Evelyn, in the previous example, had a will leaving her half-interest in the house to her son, her husband would still get full ownership of it after her death. Also, in most states, all joint tenants must own equal shares of the property.

Joint tenancy certainly has the virtue of simplicity. To create a joint tenancy, all new co-owners need to do is pay attention to the way they are listed on the document that shows ownership of property, such as a deed to real estate, a car's title slip, or the documents establishing a bank account. In the great majority of states, by calling themselves "joint tenants with the right of survivorship," the owners create a joint tenancy. In a few states, additional specific words are necessary.

CAUTION

State rules and restrictions. A few states have special rules or restrictions for joint tenancy. For example, some states require a written document that specifies a right to survivorship, and Alaska, Oregon, Tennessee, and Wisconsin each have significant restrictions on joint tenancies. Check the rules for your state before you try to set up joint tenancy ownership. If you're not comfortable researching the law on your own, a lawyer—or perhaps someone at a land title company—can help you learn the requirements.

A joint tenant can, while still alive, break the joint tenancy by transferring his or her interest in the property to someone else—or, in most states, to himself, but not as a "joint tenant." The new owner is no longer a joint tenant but owns his or her share of the property as a "tenant in common." However, if there are more than two joint tenants, the nonsevering joint tenants remain in joint tenancy with each other.

> **EXAMPLE:** Marsha, Joe, and Helen own a piece of property as joint tenants. Marsha breaks her joint tenancy by transferring her one-third interest to Dan. Dan does not become a joint tenant. He becomes a tenant in common with Joe and Helen. Joe and Helen, however, remain joint tenants between themselves.

Simultaneous Death of Joint Tenants

Many joint tenants are concerned about what will happen to their property if they die simultaneously. After all, if there's no surviving owner, the right of survivorship that's central to joint tenancy has no meaning. To deal with this highly unlikely but still potentially worrisome possibility, in your will you can name a beneficiary to inherit your share of joint tenancy property in the event that all owners die simultaneously. If you don't do this, and all the owners die simultaneously, your share will pass under your will to your residuary beneficiary (or by the laws of your state, if you don't have a will).

When to Consider Joint Tenancy—And When to Avoid It

To generalize and simplify a bit, joint tenancy can be desirable for people who buy property and want to share ownership, including inheritance rights. By contrast, it is rarely sensible for a sole owner to transfer property into joint tenancy with another simply to avoid probate of that property. Doing this creates several problems that don't occur when you pass your property using a living trust:

You can't change your mind. If you make someone else a joint tenancy owner of property that you now own yourself, you give up half-ownership of the property. The new owner has rights that you can't take back. For example, the new owner can sell or mortgage his or her share. And even if the other joint tenant's half isn't mortgaged, it could still be lost to creditors.

> **EXAMPLE:** Maureen, a widow, signs a deed that puts her house into joint tenancy with her son to avoid probate at her death. Later, the son's business fails, and his creditors sue him. Those creditors can take his half-interest in the house to pay the court judgment, which means that the house might be sold. Maureen would get the value of her half in cash; her son's half of the proceeds would go to pay the creditors.

By contrast, if you put property in a living trust, you don't give up any ownership now. You are always free to change your mind about who will get the property at your death. And your beneficiaries' creditors cannot reach the property as long as you remain alive.

There's no way to handle the incapacity of one joint tenant. If one joint tenant becomes incapacitated and cannot make decisions about the property, the other owners must get legal authority to sell it or obtain a mortgage. That may mean going to court to get someone (called a conservator, in most states) appointed to manage the incapacitated person's affairs.

With a living trust, if you (the grantor) become incapacitated, the successor trustee (or the other spouse, if it's a shared trust) takes over and has full authority to manage the trust property. No court proceedings are necessary.

Gift tax may be assessed. If you create a joint tenancy by making another person a co-owner, federal gift tax may be assessed on the transfer. If you give gifts to one person (except your spouse) exceeding $15,000 in any calendar year, you must file a gift tax return with the IRS. (See "Gift Tax," in Chapter 9.) There's one exception: If two or more people open a bank account in joint tenancy, but one person deposits all or most of the money, no gift tax is assessed against that person. A taxable gift may be made, however, when a joint tenant who has contributed little or nothing to the account withdraws money from it.

A surviving spouse could miss a tax break. If you make your spouse a joint tenant with you on property you previously owned individually, your spouse could miss out on a potentially big income tax break later if the property is sold.

With joint tenancy property, the Internal Revenue Service rule is that a surviving spouse gets what's called a "stepped-up tax basis" for only the half of the property owned by the deceased spouse. (Basis means the dollar number from which taxable profit or loss is calculated when property is sold. See the end of Chapter 9 for a discussion of stepped-up basis.) By contrast, if you leave your solely owned property to your spouse through your living trust or will, the entire property gets a stepped-up tax basis.

Tenancy by the Entirety

"Tenancy by the entirety" is a form of property ownership that is similar to joint tenancy but is limited to married couples. It is available only in the states listed below.

Tenancy by the entirety has almost the same advantages and disadvantages of joint tenancy and is most useful in the same kind of situation: when a married couple acquires property together. When one spouse dies, the surviving spouse inherits the property without probate.

If property is held in tenancy by the entirety, neither spouse can transfer his or her half of the property alone, either while alive or by will or trust. A living spouse must get the other spouse's consent to transfer the property; at death, it must go to the surviving spouse. (This is different from joint tenancy; a joint tenant is free to transfer his or her share to someone else during the joint tenant's life.)

> EXAMPLE: Fred and Ethel hold title to their apartment building in tenancy by the entirety. If Fred wanted to sell or give away his half-interest in the building, he could not do so without Ethel's signature on the deed.

States That Allow Tenancy by the Entirety

Alaska[1]	Maryland	Oklahoma
Arkansas	Massachusetts	Oregon[1,3]
Delaware	Michigan	Pennsylvania
District of Columbia[3]	Mississippi	Rhode Island[1,3]
Florida	Missouri	Tennessee
Hawaii	New Jersey[3]	Vermont
Illinois[1,3]	New York[1]	Virginia
Indiana[1]	North Carolina[1]	Wyoming
Kentucky[1]	Ohio[2]	

[1] For real estate only
[2] For real estate only, and if created before April 4, 1985
[3] Also available to registered domestic partners (DC, OR), civil unions (IL, HI, NJ, RI, VT), and reciprocal beneficiaries (HI).

Property held in tenancy by the entirety is better protected from the creditors of either spouse than is joint tenancy property from creditors of any owner. In most states, if someone sues one spouse and wins a court judgment, the creditor can't seize and sell the tenancy-by-the-entirety property to pay off the debt. (Obviously, if a creditor proves both spouses are liable for a debt, he can go after the couple's shared-ownership property, including tenancy-by-the-entirety property.) And if one spouse files for bankruptcy, creditors cannot reach or sever the property held in tenancy by the entirety.

Community Property With Right of Survivorship

Most states that allow married couples to own property as community property also allow them to agree that when one spouse dies, the deceased spouse's community property should automatically transfer to the surviving spouse without probate.

In some of these states, you can create this type of ownership by using the phrase "community property with right of survivorship" (or something similar, depending on the state) on a deed, transfer document, or account registration. If this interests you, get help from a knowledgeable estate planning attorney who can help you weigh the pros and cons of survivorship in community property. A good attorney will also know the correct terminology and formalities required by your state.

Community Property States		
Arizona	Louisiana	Texas
California*	Nevada	Washington*
Idaho	New Mexico	Wisconsin

Alaska, South Dakota, and Tennessee allow a married couple to make a written agreement stating that they wish certain property treated as community property. (See a lawyer if you want to make this kind of agreement.)

* Registered domestic partners are also covered by community property laws.

Community Property Agreements

In all community property states, married couples can choose to turn separate property into community property—this normally must be done in writing. Further, although Alaska, South Dakota, and Tennessee are not community property states, married couples who live in those states can choose to hold property as community property.

Most community property states also allow married couples to make an agreement that leaves all community property to the surviving spouse without probate. These agreements are often called "community property agreements" or CPAs.

In some states you can use a CPA to accomplish both tasks—that is, to agree that certain property (1) is community property, and (2) should pass to the surviving spouse without probate.

Each state has different rules governing its community property agreement and these agreements can be very powerful. Before you attempt to create a community property agreement yourself, it's important to really understand your state's rules and what effect your document will have. For example, you should know that because community property agreements are binding contracts, neither spouse can change or revoke them acting alone. (By contrast, you can always revoke your will.) Generally, the only ways to revoke a community property agreement are to agree to cancel (rescind) the agreement, divorce, or separate permanently. Get help from a lawyer if you have any questions or doubts.

Simplified Probate Proceedings

Many states have begun, albeit slowly, to dismantle some of the more onerous aspects of probate. As discussed in Chapter 5, most states have some form of simplified probate. What qualifies as a small estate varies from state to state, from $5,000 or less in some states to $200,000 in Wyoming.

For small estates, many states require only an affidavit procedure. By filling out a sworn statement (the affidavit) and giving it to the person who holds the property, inheritors can collect property left them by will. The beneficiary must also provide proof of his or her right to inherit, such as a death certificate and copy of the will.

RESOURCE

Learn more about probate. Get more information about probate administration, avoiding probate, and state-specific rules for simplified probate proceedings at www.nolo.com/legal-encyclopedia/executor-probate.

Life Insurance

As life insurance agents will be delighted to explain, life insurance is a good way to provide surviving family members with quick cash for debts, living expenses, and, for larger estates, estate taxes. And because you name the beneficiary in the policy itself, not in your will, life insurance proceeds don't go through probate.

The only circumstance in which life insurance proceeds are subject to probate is if the beneficiary named in the policy is your estate. That's done occasionally if the estate will need immediate cash to pay debts and taxes, but it's usually counterproductive. It's almost always a better idea to name your spouse, children, or another beneficiary who can take the money free of probate and use it to pay debts and taxes.

Although the proceeds of a life insurance policy don't go through probate, they are included in your estate for federal estate tax purposes if the person who died was the legal owner of the policy. If you think your estate might be liable for federal estate taxes, you can reduce the tax bill by giving away the policy to the beneficiary, another person, or an irrevocable life insurance trust. (See "Life Insurance Trusts," in Chapter 10.)

Choosing Life Insurance

If you're thinking about purchasing life insurance, you may feel overwhelmed by the bewildering array of policies available to you. Despite the various and confusing names for different kinds of life insurance, there are basically two types to consider for estate planning purposes: term insurance or "permanent" insurance.

Term life insurance, the less expensive type, provides insurance for a set period. For example, a five-year $150,000 policy pays the entire amount if you die within five years—and that's it. Term insurance is particularly well suited to younger parents. As a candid life insurance agent once told me, "It provides the most bang for the buck, no question." However, unlike permanent insurance, term insurance is of no value to you during your life. Also, once the term has expired, you normally have to reapply to get new life insurance.

By contrast, permanent insurance is automatically renewable. You cannot be required to take a new physical exam. And with a permanent policy, your premium payments for the years cover more than the actuarial risk of your death. The insurance company invests the excess money, and a portion of the returns is passed along to you so that the policy has a cash value to you during your lifetime.

Gifts

Here's a surprise: If you give away property while you're alive, there will be less property in your estate to go through probate when you die. While in theory you could avoid probate by giving away all your property, common sense dictates using one or more of the probate-avoidance methods discussed previously, which let you keep control over your property while you're alive.

Gifts of up to $15,000 per person per year are exempt from federal gift tax. (See "Making Gifts During Life," in Chapter 10.) ●

Retirement Plans as Estate Planning Devices

R etirement plans, which may compose a big part of your savings, can function as estate planning devices. In particular, if you have an individual retirement program such as an IRA, 401(k), or profit-sharing plan, these can hold significant amounts of money if you die prematurely. Any money left in a retirement account is part of your estate. With any individual retirement program, you name one or more beneficiaries to receive any money left in the account when you die. The money goes directly to your beneficiaries and is not subject to probate.

Before we look further into how you can use your retirement plans in estate planning, it's important to note that these devices are not primarily intended to provide money to beneficiaries. They are designed to provide money to you, the owner, in your retirement. Because of this, federal law requires that after you reach age 70½ you must withdraw at least a certain portion of your retirement account every year or face a monetary penalty. (Roth IRAs function differently. See "Roth IRAs," below.) The withdrawal amount is recalculated every year, based on your current life expectancy and, to some extent, that of your beneficiary. So if you live to a ripe old age, there will be no or very little money left in your account when you die. Thus, for estate planning purposes, these accounts are not fixed assets, like a house, which you can reasonably count on to retain (at least) their full present value.

RESOURCE

Information on retirement planning. When they retire, most people are entitled to payments from one or more retirement programs, such as Social Security, military benefits, private or public employee pensions, union pension plans, or individual retirement accounts. Planning for a financially comfortable retirement can be complicated, and I don't pretend to address that subject here. There are numerous books, magazines, websites, and proclaimed experts who can give you all the advice you may want, and then some. Here are some good resources available from Nolo:

- *IRAs, 401(k)s & Other Retirement Plans: Strategies for Taking Your Money Out*, by Twila Slesnick and John C. Suttle
- *Long-Term Care: How to Plan & Pay for It*, by Joseph Matthews, and
- *Social Security, Medicare & Government Pensions: Get the Most Out of Your Retirement & Medical Benefits*, by Joseph Matthews.

You can also visit Nolo's website, at www.nolo.com, to learn more about planning for retirement.

Individual Retirement Programs

In addition to Social Security, savings, and investments, many people contribute regularly to one or more individual retirement programs that will assure them an income when they get older.

Traditional Individual Retirement Programs

Individual retirement programs such as regular IRAs (individual retirement accounts), profit-sharing plans (formerly called Keogh plans), and SEP-IRAs (IRAs for small businesses and the self-employed) are retirement plans you fund yourself. The money you contribute is tax deductible, within limits. You are in charge of how the money is invested. You don't pay tax on any earnings, either, in the year earned. After you retire, when you withdraw money from the account, that money is taxable income in the year you get it.

Any income earner can create a regular IRA by making annual contributions. The annual contribution limit for 2020 is $6,000 for those up to age 50. For those age 50 or older, the annual limit is $7,000. The deduction amount rises in $500 increments based on the rate of inflation.

The contribution limit for a profit-sharing plan or a SEP-IRA is a percentage of net income, and can be well over $40,000.

RESOURCE

More information about individual retirement programs.
IRS Publication 590-A, *Contributions to Individual Retirement Arrangements (IRAs)*, and IRS Publication 590-B, *Distributions from Individual Retirement Arrangements (IRAs)*, provide detailed (and complex) information on IRAs. IRS Publication 560, *Retirement Plans for Small Business*, covers retirement plans for the self-employed, such as SEP-IRAs. You can download these publications for free by visiting the IRS's website at www.irs.gov.

Roth IRAs

The Roth IRA differs from the traditional IRA in several respects. You fund a Roth IRA with money that has already been taxed. Annual contribution amounts are the same as those for traditional IRAs, described above. (By contrast, the money you place in a regular IRA is tax deductible in the year contributed.) All earnings from money in a Roth IRA are tax-free. And when you withdraw money, no further income tax is due as long as the money was in the account for at least five years.

The biggest difference, for estate planning purposes, between regular IRAs (and most other retirement plans) and a Roth IRA is that you don't have to start withdrawing money from a Roth IRA when you reach age 70½. So, if you choose, you can leave all of a Roth IRA untouched when you die—and this money will pass to your named beneficiary, free of probate.

401(k) or 403(b) Plans

Many employers offer employees what are called 401(k) plans and 403(b) plans. (The 401(k) is for businesses, the 403(b) is for nonprofit corporations.) Under these plans employees can, if they choose, defer a portion of their pretax wages, having them paid instead into the retirement program. Some employers match these funds or at least make some contribution to the account.

Money in your account is invested, and you hope the investments prosper. (We've all learned that 401(k) growth is not a law of nature.) All funds in the account are tax-free until you withdraw them. As with an IRA, you must begin withdrawing money from the account at age 70½, based on your life expectancy. The amount you must withdraw is recalculated every year. At your death, the beneficiary you've named receives whatever funds are left in the account, without probate. If you are married, the beneficiary must be your surviving spouse unless your spouse signed an agreement giving up this right. (See "Choosing Beneficiaries for Individual Retirement Programs," below.)

Money in a deceased person's pension plan or personal retirement account can be "rolled over" into an IRA of a named beneficiary. Personal retirement accounts include IRAs, SEP-IRAs, and 401(k) and 403(b) plans. The "rollover" provision allows the beneficiary to withdraw funds from the new IRA account based on the beneficiary's life expectancy. The beneficiary must start making withdrawals in the year the funds are received. But if, as is often the case, the beneficiary is significantly younger than the deceased person was, the withdrawals can be spread over many years. This can substantially reduce the overall income taxes paid on the money received, compared to the tax that would have to be paid if the beneficiary received the money in one lump sum.

Pensions

A pension, unlike an individual retirement program, is not under your control. Your company sets up a pension plan and determines what rights you receive. You may acquire the right to receive payments—perhaps generous ones—and this right may extend to your spouse after you die. But what you have are rights to benefits, not ownership of assets, as you have with an individual retirement program. Your right to leave any of your pension benefits to beneficiaries is determined by the plan.

No law requires an employer to offer a pension plan. And there's no legal requirement that a pension plan pay benefits to any beneficiary. Some are generous; some provide nothing after the employee dies.

RESOURCE

More information about pension plans. IRS Publication 575, *Pension and Annuity Income*, discusses the rules for many pension plans, but it's not easy reading. You can download it for free from the IRS website, at www.irs.gov. A number of brochures on pensions, which are easier to understand, are available from The American Association of Retired Persons (AARP), 601 E Street NW, Washington, DC 20049, 888-687-2277, www.aarp.org, and the Pension Rights Center, 1730 M St. NW, Suite 1000, Washington, DC 20036, 888-420-6550, www.pensionrights.org.

Choosing Beneficiaries for Individual Retirement Programs

If you have an individual retirement program, it may contain a substantial amount of money when you die. (Sadly, the earlier you die after age 70, the more money the retirement program is likely to have.) Choosing who will inherit any remaining funds may be one of the most important estate planning decisions you make.

You should always name a beneficiary for an individual retirement program, such as an IRA, Roth IRA, profit-sharing, or 401(k) plan. Except for 401(k) or 403(b) plans, you can name more than one beneficiary if you like. Indeed, you can name many beneficiaries, with any money left in the account divided among them as you specify. You can also name alternate beneficiaries for each primary beneficiary.

The one big exception to your freedom to name beneficiaries is that if you're legally married, you *must* name your spouse as sole beneficiary of your 401(k) or 403(b) program, unless your spouse waives his or her right. This can become an important, and sensitive, matter.

> **EXAMPLE:** Arlette is in her mid-40s, has a well-paying job in computer graphics, and has a 14-year-old daughter. Arlette's one major asset is a chunk of money in her company's 401(k) program. Long divorced, Arlette wants to marry Adam. But she does not want him to be the beneficiary of her 401(k) program; she wants the beneficiary to continue to be her daughter. It may require some tact for Arlette to successfully explain to her fiancé why she's asking him to sign a waiver of his rights to the 401(k) shortly before the marriage.

Also, in community property states, each spouse has a legal half-interest in money that the other spouse has earned during the marriage, unless that spouse signs a document giving up the interest. (This waiver is accomplished in a separate document from that which waives 401(k) inheritance rights.)

In reality, many married people do name their spouses as the beneficiaries of their individual retirement program. They want to support their spouses, and for larger estates, defer possible estate tax. (Leaving assets to the surviving spouse postpones tax, under the marital deduction, until the death of that spouse. See "Property You Leave to Your Spouse," in Chapter 9.) But as long as you don't run afoul of laws requiring retirement program money to be left to a spouse, you can name anyone you want as beneficiary. For one reason or another, some people do name a child or other person as beneficiary.

Retirement Plans and Taxes

All money you leave in an individual retirement program—for example, the remaining balance in an IRA, Roth IRA, or 401(k) plan—is subject to federal estate tax when you die. It doesn't matter how the funds are paid out, whether in a lump sum or over time. The dollar value of the account at death is part of your estate for estate-tax purposes. Whether tax will actually have to be paid depends on the net value of your entire estate, and perhaps the year of death. Currently, only very large estates owe federal estate tax, but in a few states even those with moderate estates need to keep an eye out for state estate taxes. (See Chapter 9.)

Also, the beneficiary will have to pay income tax on any money left in most retirement plans. (This is not the case with most other inherited assets.) These tax payments are assessed because when the money was first socked away, the contributions were tax deductible, as was any money the account earned. Now that the money is withdrawn, the taxman wants his cut, regardless of the death of the person who created the account. However, a surviving spouse may be able to "roll over" money from a deceased spouse's IRA into his or her own IRA and not have the money subject to income tax until he or she makes withdrawals from that account.

Money in a Roth IRA is not subject to income tax when the beneficiary inherits it. That's because money contributed to a Roth IRA is taxed when made; the IRS has already taken its bite. Also, any earnings from contributions that have been in the account for at least five years are not taxed when withdrawn by the inheritor. However, money earned in the account after the initial depositor's death is subject to income tax. ●

Estate Tax

A fter some years of uncertainty, Congress has settled on long-term laws for federal estate taxes. The two basic rules are:

- Every person has a personal exemption from federal estate tax. The personal exemption for 2020 is $11.58 million. This amount increases each year based on the annual rate of inflation.
- All property left to a surviving spouse is exempt from federal estate taxes.

These two rules mean that very, very few estates will have to pay any federal estate tax. Indeed, the vast majority of estates—99.9%—do not pay any federal estate taxes. If tax must be paid, the tax rate starts at 40%.

Additionally, a few states impose an inheritance tax on the property of a deceased person who lived or owned real estate in that state. And a handful of states levy their own state estate taxes that apply in addition to state inheritance taxes and federal estate taxes.

No Income Tax on Inherited Property

Because many people worry about this, I want to state explicitly that people who inherit property do not currently have to pay income or capital gains tax on the worth of the property. (One exception is funds in most individual retirement accounts; see "Retirement Plans and Taxes," in Chapter 8.) However, after a person inherits property, any income subsequently received from the property is regular income and is subject to income tax.

Federal Estate Tax Exemptions

Several federal tax law exemptions and deductions allow you to leave substantial amounts of property free of estate tax. The most important of these are:

The personal exemption. This exemption allows you to leave property worth up to $11.58 million free of estate tax, no matter to whom you leave the property. If you have made taxable gifts during your life, the amount of the personal exemption will be reduced accordingly. (See "Gift Tax," below.)

The marital deduction. This exemption allows you to leave any amount of property to your spouse tax-free. This exemption applies only to surviving spouses who are citizens of the United States.

The charitable deduction. This exempts all property you leave to a tax-exempt charity. (See "Gifts to Charities," below.)

"Portability." The personal exemption of $11.58 million is "portable" between spouses. Whatever portion of the personal estate-tax exemption not used by the first spouse to die, can be "ported" over to the second spouse.

> EXAMPLE: Lance and Buffy have an estate worth $18 million. Lance dies in 2019, leaving his half, or $9 million, to Buffy. All the property Lance leaves to Buffy is exempt from tax because of the marital deduction. So Lance's estate uses up none of his 2019 $11.4 million personal exemption. Buffy's estate is now worth $18 million. She dies in 2020. None of her $18 million is subject to estate tax because her estate can combine her $11.58 million personal exemption with Lance's unused exemption, making her total exemption nearly $23 million.

These exemptions and deductions mean that all but the super-rich will escape estate taxes. Whether this is wise policy depends on one's views on inherited wealth.

RESOURCE
Keep tabs on changes to the estate tax. Although federal estate tax laws are currently stable, political changes in Congress could lead to changes, including reductions in the amount of the personal estate-tax exemption. You can keep up to date on this, and how such a change could affect *state* estate tax, at www.nolo.com/legal-encyclopedia/estate-tax.

Property You Leave to Your Spouse

As discussed above, the marital deduction allows you to leave property to your spouse free of federal estate tax. You must be legally married to qualify for the marital deduction. There are no similar exemptions for unmarried couples.

> **EXAMPLE:** Pamela dies in 2020. She leaves $23 million to her husband, Rinaldo. No estate tax is assessed.

The marital deduction works in addition to all other allowable estate tax deductions.

> **EXAMPLE:** Marty has an estate valued at $10 million. He leaves $4 million to his children and the rest, $6 million, to his wife. Marty dies in 2020. All Marty's property is exempt from federal estate tax—the $6 million because of the marital deduction and the remaining $4 million because it is below the $11.58 million personal estate tax exemption for 2020.

Special Rules for Noncitizen Spouses

No marital deduction is allowed for property left by one spouse to a spouse who is not a citizen of the United States. It doesn't matter that a noncitizen spouse was married to a U.S. citizen or is a legal resident of the United States. The surviving spouse must be a U.S. citizen to be eligible for the marital deduction. (On the other hand, property a noncitizen spouse leaves to a citizen spouse is eligible for the marital deduction.)

Why this discrimination against noncitizen spouses? Congress feared that noncitizen spouses would leave the United States after the death of their citizen spouses, whisking away their wealth to foreign lands so it would never be subject to U.S. tax.

Fortunately, you can still leave your noncitizen spouse a good deal of property free of estate tax. The personal estate tax exemption can be used for property left to a noncitizen spouse, as well as to anyone else. So a substantial amount of property—currently over $11 million—can be left tax-free to a noncitizen spouse.

Congress has provided one way that a spouse can leave property to a noncitizen spouse and obtain additional estate tax protection. The marital deduction applies to property left to a noncitizen spouse in what's called a Qualified Domestic Trust (or QDOT).

> **EXAMPLE:** Giuseppe is married to Dominique, a noncitizen. Giuseppe dies with an estate of $12 million in 2021. He leaves his estate to Dominique in a QDOT trust. No taxes are due when he dies. The property in the QDOT trust qualifies for the marital deduction.

SEE AN EXPERT

Creating a QDOT trust. To prepare one of these trusts, you'll need a lawyer. QDOT trusts are tricky, and you need to understand all the estate tax consequences, including the fact that your property will eventually be taxed on its worth when your spouse dies, as part of that estate, not what it is worth when you die, as part of your estate.

Gifts to Charities

All gifts you leave to tax-exempt charitable organizations are exempt from federal tax.

If you are wealthy, you may want to explore a "charitable remainder trust" for making gifts to charities. With a charitable remainder trust, you make a gift to a charity while you live, and then receive a certain annual income from the gift property during your life—either a fixed-dollar amount or a fixed percentage of the annual net worth of the gift asset. There are income tax, as well as estate tax, benefits that flow from a charitable remainder trust. (See "Tax-Saving Irrevocable Trusts," in Chapter 10.)

Taxes in Estate Planning

In estate planning, there are a few different taxes that you'll need to consider. Here's a quick-fix guide to the basics.

Federal Estate Tax. A tax imposed by the federal government on the estate of the deceased based on the overall size of the estate. Currently only estates worth well over $11 million owe this tax.

State Estate Tax. A tax imposed by a state government on the estate of the deceased based on the overall size of the estate. The personal exemption and tax rate vary by state.

Inheritance Tax. A state tax imposed on a decedent's estate by a handful of states on property owned by state residents and all real estate located in the state.

Gift Tax. A tax imposed at death on gratuitous transfers of property (gifts) made during life if the total amount of gifts made during your life and at death is greater than the personal exemption for the year of death. A federal exclusion permits limited annual gifts of $15,000 per beneficiary that do not count against your lifetime gift total.

State Estate and Inheritance Tax

There are two types of *state* taxes that may be imposed on the property you leave: inheritance tax and state estate tax. If you live in a state that imposes one of these taxes, and your estate is large enough to be taxed, there is little you can do to avoid the tax, except move to another state that does not impose tax. This is rarely a viable option.

Inheritance tax. Just a handful of states impose a traditional inheritance tax on property left by a deceased person. These states are Iowa, Kentucky, Maryland, Nebraska, New Jersey, and Pennsylvania. Inheritance tax is imposed on:

- all property of residents of the state, no matter where the property is located, and

- all real estate located in the state, no matter where the deceased resided.

State estate tax. A number of states have their own estate tax, separate from the federal estate tax. If you live in one of these states, it's possible that your estate will owe taxes to both the state and federal governments. Like the federal estate tax, each state allows a personal exemption that prevents many estates from owing tax. However, the states' exemptions are all significantly lower than the federal exemption. So it is possible for an estate to owe state estate tax even if it doesn't owe federal estate tax. The tax rates for state estate taxes are relatively low—10%–20%, compared to the 40% federal estate tax rate.

SEE AN EXPERT

Learning your state's inheritance and estate tax rules. If you are concerned about your state's tax laws, see a lawyer or tax professional who can bring you up to date on this ever-changing area of the law. Also, Nolo provides state-specific information online at www.nolo.com/legal-encyclopedia/estate-tax.

Gift Tax

The federal government imposes a tax on substantial gifts made during life. This tax came about because Congress reasoned that if only property left at death were taxed, people would give away as much property as they could during their lives, effectively voiding the estate tax laws. So gift tax rates are the same as estate tax rates, to eliminate any tax incentive for making large gifts. The tax is imposed on the giver of the gift, not the recipient and the personal exemption for estate taxes is actually a combined exemption with the gift tax. In 2020, this combined exemption is $11.58 million. (And this amount will rise with inflation in future years.) In other words, if you add together the taxable gifts you make during life with the taxable gifts you leave at death, you can pass over $11 million, without owing gift or estate taxes.

If you make a taxable gift during your life, you do not pay any tax at that time unless you have exceeded your lifetime federal estate tax exemption. That's highly unlikely. For example, if you made a taxable gift of $100,000 in 2020, you would pay gift tax only if you had previously given taxable gifts totaling over $11.48 million. Instead, the amount of the taxable gift will be deducted from your estate tax exemption after your death.

> **EXAMPLE:** Jerry gives Hamid a gift, $500,000 of which is subject to gift tax. Jerry cannot pay the tax on that amount now. Instead, the $500,000 will be deducted from the amount of his personal estate tax exemption when he dies. Jerry dies in 2020, when the personal exemption is $11.58 million, so his estate tax exemption becomes $11.08 million.

There are several important exceptions to the gift tax rules: the annual exemption, the marital exemption, and an exemption for gifts to cover medical bills or school expenses. In this section, I'll discuss each in turn.

The Annual Exemption

Federal law exempts (technically, it's called an "exclusion") a set dollar value of gifts from tax. In 2020, you can give up to $15,000 per calendar year per beneficiary free of gift tax.

> **EXAMPLE:** Suno gives each of her five children $15,000 in 2020. All of these gifts are tax exempt.

Both members of a couple have separate $15,000 exemptions, so they can give a combined total of $30,000 per beneficiary per year tax free.

> **EXAMPLE:** In 2020, Elliot and Gina give $30,000 to their daughter, $30,000 more to their daughter's husband, and $30,000 to each of their daughter's three children. All these gifts are tax exempt.

As this example shows, over time, wealthy people can give away large amounts of money tax free. Elliot and Gina gave away $150,000 tax free in one year. Multiply that sum by, say, five years, and you get an idea of just how much can be removed from a wealthy estate by an extensive gift-giving program.

The $15,000 gift tax exemption is indexed yearly based on inflation. As inflation increases the gift tax exemption rises in increments of $1,000 rounded down to the lower thousand. In other words, inflation increases must cumulatively raise the current exemption by more than $1,000 before the gift tax exemption is raised to $16,000.

The Marital Exemption

All gifts between spouses are exempt from gift tax, no matter how much the gift property is worth. This rule is part of the marital deduction discussed above.

The marital deduction does not apply to gifts from a citizen spouse to a noncitizen spouse. In 2020, the rule here is that gifts worth up to $157,000 per year can be made to a noncitizen spouse, tax free.

Gifts for Medical Bills or School Tuition

If you pay someone else's medical bills or school tuition, your gift is tax exempt. This exemption has a couple of twists, however. First, you must pay the money directly to the provider of the medical service or the school. If you give the money to an ill person or student, who then pays the bill, the gift is not tax exempt. Nor can you reimburse someone who has already paid a medical or tuition bill and receive the tax exemption. Finally, you cannot get the exemption for payments covering a student's other educational expenses, such as room and board.

The Federal Income-Tax Basis of Inherited Property

Though it's not, strictly speaking, an estate tax matter, the question of how inherited property is valued for the purpose of calculating gain or loss from a subsequent sale is closely related, and important to many people. Generally, if you own property that has significantly increased in value since you bought it, it's desirable from a tax standpoint to leave that property to others when you die, rather than to sell it or give it away during your life. To understand why this is so, we have to take a little jaunt into tax land.

Let's start with a definition. The word "basis" means the value assigned to property from which taxable gain or loss on sale is determined. The concept of a property's basis is a tricky one, not made any easier by the fact that "basis" is not defined in the tax laws. When property is purchased, its basis is generally its cost. In fact, basis is often referred to as "cost basis." For example, if you buy some stock for $5,000, it has a basis equal to its cost—$5,000. If you sell the stock two months later for $16,000 (lucky you), your taxable profit is $11,000.

Sale Price	*$16,000*
Minus Basis	*– $ 5,000*
Taxable Gain	*$11,000*

The original cost basis can be adjusted up, for certain types of improvements to property, or down, for reasons like depreciation. For instance, if you make what's called a "capital improvement" to a house, such as putting in a new foundation, the cost of the improvement is added to the basis of the property. A capital improvement can be very roughly defined as an improvement that lasts more than a year.

EXAMPLE: Green Is Good, Inc., buys an old barn in which to design and make bicycles. The barn costs the company $270,000, so it has a cost basis of $270,000. Over the next year, Green Is Good spends $230,000 for capital improvements to the barn, installing a new fire-control system and a new roof. Here's how the company determines the adjusted basis:

Original Cost	*$270,000*
Plus Capital Improvements	*+ $230,000*
Adjusted Basis	*$500,000*

On its income tax return, the company takes depreciation deductions of $30,000 for the barn. The property's adjusted basis is now $470,000, because the deduction for depreciation lowers the adjusted basis of the property.

After several years, Green Is Good needs a larger production plant. It sells the barn for $700,000 to The Mogul Company, which plans to convert the barn into rental apartments for skiers.

Green Is Good determines its profit this way:

Sale Price	*$700,000*
Minus Basis	*– $470,000*
Taxable Profit	*$230,000*

The Mogul Company's basis in the barn is $700,000.

Now to move to the tax basis of inherited property. Under federal tax law, the basis of inherited property is "stepped-up" to its fair market value at the date of the deceased owner's death. Actually, this is a simplification of the rule, which is that the basis of inherited property is adjusted *up or down* to the market value as of the date of death. However, the assumption that prices of property rise over time is so ingrained in our economic life that the term commonly used is "stepped-up" basis. And in practice, for property owned for a long period of time, the inheritor's basis—the net value of the property at death of the previous owner—is almost always higher than that of the previous owner.

> **EXAMPLE:** The Mogul Company is solely owned by I. B. Wily. In five years of ownership, he spends $350,000 turning the barn into apartments, and takes $150,000 total depreciation. His basis in the building is calculated as follows:
>
> | | |
> |---|---|
> | *Purchase Price* | *$700,000* |
> | *Plus Capital Improvements* | *+ $350,000* |
> | *Minus Depreciation* | *– $150,000* |
> | *Adjusted Basis* | *$900,000* |
>
> After his fifth year of ownership, Mr. Wily dies, leaving the building to his daughter, Ursula. At his death, the building is valued at $1.5 million. Ursula's basis in the building is "stepped-up" to this $1.5 million.

The fact that the basis of property is stepped up to its fair market value at the owner's death means that it's almost always desirable to hold on to appreciated property until it can pass at death. That way, your inheritors obtain the advantage of the stepped-up basis rule. Thus, if Wily sold the building for $1.5 million shortly before he died, he would have had to pay federal capital gains taxes (and probably state capital gains taxes as well) on $600,000 ($1.5 million sale price minus his $900,000 basis). By contrast, if Wily left the building to Ursula and she sold it for $1.5 million, no tax would be assessed.

Gifts made during life are not entitled to a stepped-up basis. Only transfers at death qualify for this desirable tax treatment. So if Wily gave the property to Ursula a few weeks before he died, her basis would be $900,000.

The Tax Basis of Joint Tenancy Property

With joint tenancy property, only the portion owned by the deceased owner gets a stepped-up basis. The portion owned by surviving joint tenants continues to have the same basis it had before.

EXAMPLE: Colette and Marion buy an apartment house in joint tenancy, each contributing half the purchase price of $400,000. Each person's share has a basis of $200,000. Five years later, Colette dies, and the apartment house has a net value of $800,000. The basis of Colette's half-interest in the property is stepped up to $400,000 from $200,000. But Marion's share retains its basis of $200,000.

Because the property was owned in joint tenancy, Marion, of course, receives Colette's share. Here is Marion's basis in the property:

Marion's Share	*$200,000*
Colette's Share	*+$400,000*
Net Basis	*$600,000*

Two years later, Marion sells the apartment house for $850,000.
Here is Marion's profit, for capital gains tax purposes:

Sale Price	*$850,000*
Minus Marion's Basis	*−$600,000*
Profit	*$250,000*

Reducing Federal Estate Taxes

What can you do to reduce federal estate taxes if you think your estate will be liable for them? Not as much as you might hope. Of course, for the extremely rich, high-priced experts do come up with ingenious, or twisted, ways to dodge taxes. For those who are merely wealthy, aside from making use of the estate tax exemptions and deductions discussed in Chapter 9, there are basically only a few ways to reduce estate tax: make gifts during your life, use a disclaimer trust, or use an irrevocable trust. This chapter discusses these options.

Making Gifts During Life

Obviously, if you give away property while you live, that removes the value of that property from your taxable estate. Here we'll look at different types of gifts you may want to make.

Using the Federal Gift Tax Exclusion

As you know from the discussion in Chapter 9, you can make gifts worth up to $15,000 per person per calendar year free of gift tax. A couple can give $30,000 per year tax free to any person. Tax-exempt gift giving can remove large amounts of money from an estate. A gift-giving program can be particularly advantageous for wealthy folks who have several children, grandchildren, or other people they'd like to help.

You can also make tax-free gifts of any amount for:
- payments made for someone's educational or medical costs, and
- contributions to tax-exempt charities. If you're quite prosperous, you may want to look into what's called a "charitable remainder trust."

To learn more about reducing your estate by making these types of tax-free gifts, see "Gift Tax," in Chapter 9.

Gifts of Interests in a Family Business

Gifts of minority interests in a family business can, in the right circumstances, reduce estate taxes. This is because a minority interest can be valued, for gift tax purposes, at less than the value it would have if it were part of the majority interest.

> EXAMPLE: Angela gives her daughter, Lucia, 10% of Angela's interest in her furniture company. At the time of the gift, the company is worth $1 million. The value put on Lucia's 10% share is not $100,000 but something significantly less, in the $60,000–$80,000 range, because of minority business discounts. (The accounting rules here are fuzzy, and a tax professional must be consulted.)

Though this method can be helpful for an existing business, it's unlikely to work if you try to create a business and place your major assets, such as your home, in it. Under IRS rules, a family business must serve a valid business purpose and cannot be designed solely or primarily to reduce estate taxes.

Some "experts" have touted one particular business form, called a "family limited partnership," as a wonderful device for eliminating estate taxes. There's nothing at all magical about this type of business. It cannot transmute nonbusiness assets into a valid family business.

SEE AN EXPERT

Reducing taxes on a family business. If you have a family business and believe your estate may be liable for estate tax, see a lawyer to learn your options for reducing the tax bite.

Gifts of Life Insurance

From an estate tax standpoint, it can be very desirable to give away life insurance during your life. If you own your life insurance policy at your death, the proceeds (death payment) are included in your taxable estate. If the policy has a large death benefit—say, hundreds of thousands of dollars or more—including that sum in your taxable estate can result in substantial federal estate taxes. But the proceeds will not be subject to tax if someone else owns the policy when you die.

> **CAUTION**
>
> **Don't wait to make a gift of life insurance.** Under IRS regulations, a gift of life insurance must be made at least three years before your death. The potential tax savings from making a gift of life insurance are so large that the IRS will not allow any "deathbed" gifts. Defining "last minute" to mean at least three years does seem a tad excessive, but it's pointless to quarrel with the tax folks over this one.

Gifts of life insurance are subject to gift tax. The worth of the gift is, basically, the current value of the policy. This will always be far less than the amount the policy will pay at your death. If the present value is under $15,000, no gift tax will be assessed.

There are two ways you can transfer ownership of a life insurance policy. First, you can simply give the policy to another person or persons. Your life insurance company should have an assignment form you can use to accomplish this. Second, you can create an irrevocable life insurance trust, and transfer ownership to that entity. You'd create a trust if there's no person to whom you want to assign the policy outright. (See "Life Insurance Trusts," below, for a fuller explanation of why you might want a trust.)

Transferring ownership of your policy to another person or a trust involves a trade-off: Once the policy is transferred, you've lost all power over it, forever. You cannot cancel it or change the beneficiary. To make this point bluntly, suppose you transfer ownership of your policy to your spouse, and later get divorced. You cannot cancel the policy or recover it from your now ex-spouse. Nevertheless, in many situations, the trade-off is worth it—for example, when you transfer policy ownership to a child or children with whom you have a close and loving relationship.

Disclaimer Trusts

Another approach to possibly saving on estate taxes—for very wealthy couples—is to prepare a "disclaimer trust." A disclaimer is a device specifically authorized by federal law that allows any one to decline to receive property left to him or her. Put simply, you cannot be compelled to accept a gift or an inheritance, if you decide it's better that it go elsewhere. When a gift is disclaimed, it goes to whoever is next in line to receive it. With a living trust, disclaimed property goes to the alternate beneficiary defined in the trust document.

With a disclaimer trust, a couple each leaves her or his property to the other, but with an express provision that if the surviving spouse disclaims any portion or all of the deceased spouse's trust property, that property goes into a separate, irrevocable trust.

Why would a surviving spouse want to disclaim property? For married couples, it might make tax sense if Congress reduces the amount of the personal exemption or repeals "portability."

Let's take one hypothetical. Suppose that for 2021 and thereafter, Congress leaves the exemption at over $11 million but eliminates the "portability" provision of the current law. So the unused portion of a deceased spouse's tax exemption could not be "ported" to the surviving spouse's estate. Claudia and James have a co-owned estate of $14 million. Each leaves all their property to the other. James dies in 2021. His $7 million goes to Claudia and her estate is now worth $14 million. She dies in 2023. Because under this hypothetical she (her estate) cannot "port" any of James's estate tax exemption, Claudia's estate would be subject to federal estate tax. The amount subject to tax would be $14 million minus the estate tax exemption for 2023.

Enter the disclaimer trust. If Claudia and James had set up a disclaimer trust, she could have disclaimed $3 million of his estate. That $3 million would have gone to an irrevocable trust, with Claudia as the trust beneficiary. Property that goes into it is subject to estate tax, but James's exemption of over $11 million exemption is applied, so no tax is due. Claudia's estate is now worth $11 million, so no tax will be due on her estate when she dies either.

Disclaimer trusts can be especially desirable for wealthy unmarried couples because only married couples can use portability. For *unmarried* couples, when the first partner dies and leaves everything directly to the second partner, the second partner ends up with a very large estate, but the estate tax exemption of only one person. (Unlike their married counterparts who would have two exemptions to use.)

> EXAMPLE: Peter and Alan have been partners for many decades. Peter has assets worth $6 million. Alan has assets worth $9 million. Each wants to leave his property to the other. Without a disclaimer trust, if Peter dies first, Alan will be left with an estate of $15 million—over the estate tax exemption. When Alan dies, his estate will owe taxes on that overage.
>
> To avoid this tax, Peter and Alan each create a disclaimer trust that leaves his property to the other. When Peter dies, Alan disclaims just enough of Alan's property to keep his estate under the estate tax exemption. The disclaimed property goes into an irrevocable trust. Alan has the right to use the property in that trust, but never becomes the legal owner of that property. When Alan dies, his estate does not owe tax because he has kept it under the amount of the estate tax exemption.

Disclaimer trusts are a form of insurance, or prudent preparation, for wealthy couples. If the estate tax law is changed significantly, a couple with a disclaimer trust has protected themselves as best they can from any negative impact of those changes. If there's no tax reason to disclaim, the surviving spouse simply accepts the deceased spouse's property. Simply put, there's no serious downside to having a disclaimer trust.

Clearly, a disclaimer trust is not for everyone. A couple's combined estate must be near or over the estate tax-exempt amount before they could need a disclaimer trust to avoid federal estate taxes. Under current law, that exempt amount is over $11 million, so federal estate taxes are a non-issue for most people. Further, Congress could eliminate the federal estate tax altogether. In that case, however, you could still use a disclaimer trust to avoid state estate taxes, in the handful of states that have them.

Disclaimer Trusts and State Estate Taxes

Even if you're not worried about federal estate taxes, you may be able to use a disclaimer trust to eliminate or reduce state estate taxes if:

- you live in a state with a state estate tax
- your state's personal exemption is relatively low
- your estate may be worth more than the exemption, and
- you have a spouse or partner.

If you think this rather narrow set of circumstances might apply to you, get help from an attorney to discuss whether using a disclaimer trust could guard against state estate taxes when the second spouse or partner dies. (See Chapter 9 for more about state estate taxes.)

Tax-Saving Irrevocable Trusts

There are also several types of irrevocable trusts that can be useful for very wealthy couples who want to save on estate taxes.

SEE AN EXPERT

Preparing an irrevocable estate tax-saving trust. An attorney must prepare any of the estate tax-saving trusts discussed in this section. IRS regulations applicable to irrevocable trusts are complicated. A mistake can cost your inheritors all the tax savings you planned for, and then some. Also, irrevocable trusts are designed to function for relatively long periods of time, which means that there must be careful consideration of contingencies that may arise. Drafting such a trust is difficult. This section gives you an overview; if you want to learn more about the basics of irrevocable estate tax-saving trusts before you see a lawyer, consult *Plan Your Estate*, by Denis Clifford (Nolo).

The QTIP Trust for Married Couples

A QTIP (Qualified Terminable Interest Property) trust is used to postpone, not eliminate or reduce, payment of estate tax. It is normally used when a spouse's individual estate exceeds the estate tax threshold.

> EXAMPLE: Maxine has an estate worth $13 million. She dies in 2020, when the estate tax exemption is $11.58 million. Over $1 million of her estate would be subject to tax.

With an estate "overage," a spouse can postpone tax by leaving all this overage to the surviving spouse. (Remember, all property left to a surviving spouse is exempt under the marital deduction.) But a spouse may want neither to have his or her estate pay taxes when he or she dies, nor to leave any overage to the surviving spouse. Commonly, this is because the spouse wants his or her property to go eventually to his or her children or other inheritors.

Here's where a QTIP trust can be helpful: With a QTIP, the surviving spouse must be left use of the trust property for life. But property in the QTIP trust qualifies for the marital deduction. In other words, QTIP trust property isn't subject to tax when the spouse who created the trust dies. Also—and this is often key—with a QTIP, the spouse who sets it up gets to name the final beneficiaries. When the surviving spouse dies, the QTIP trust property goes to whomever the trust creator chooses to inherit it.

> EXAMPLE: Maxine, who is wealthy, has recently married her fourth husband, James. She has three children from her first two marriages. In her

estate plan, she leaves an amount equal to the estate tax exemption for the year of her death to be divided equally among her three children. For the balance of her property, she creates a QTIP trust, with James as the life beneficiary and her three children as the final beneficiaries. When Maxine dies, James is still alive. No estate tax will be assessed as long as he lives.

Estate tax is assessed on property in a QTIP trust when the surviving spouse (the life beneficiary) dies. The trust property is counted as part of the surviving spouse's estate. Here we reach the main drawback of QTIP trusts. When taxes are assessed, the property in the trust is valued at what it is worth when the surviving spouse dies, not what it was worth when the first spouse died. If the value of the trust property has significantly increased, this can mean a higher tax bill.

EXAMPLE: In 2012, Jane left property worth $5 million in her QTIP. Her husband, Max (the life beneficiary), dies in 2020, with an estate worth $800,000, plus the value of the QTIP property. In just eight years, the value of the QTIP property increased from $5 million to $12 million. The full $12 million is included in Max's taxable estate.

Deciding whether to use a QTIP is a complex matter. I've just scratched the surface here; using QTIPs can get much more complicated. For example, there is a "reverse QTIP election," which can be used to divide part of the property originally scheduled for a QTIP into two parts, only one of which goes into the trust. But I won't burden you with an explanation of how a reverse QTIP election works—or with the particulars of other sophisticated uses of this type of trust. If you've got a lot of money, see a good estate planning lawyer to find out whether a QTIP is something you want.

Life Insurance Trusts

An irrevocable life insurance trust is a legal entity that owns life insurance you previously owned. You create a life insurance trust and transfer your insurance policy to the trust.

Once you transfer ownership of life insurance, the trust owns the policy, not you. That means the proceeds aren't part of your estate and can't be subject to estate tax.

Why bother to create a life insurance trust, when you can remove insurance proceeds from your estate simply by giving ownership of the policy to someone else? Usually, because there's no adult to whom you want to give your policy. In other words, you want to get the proceeds out of your taxable estate, but you want the legal control over the policy that a trust can offer. For example, the trust can specify that the policy must be kept in effect while you live, eliminating the risk that a new owner of the policy could decide to cash it in.

> **EXAMPLE:** Judith is the divorced mother of two children in their 20s, who will be her beneficiaries. Neither is sensible with money. Judith has an estate worth $11 million, plus a life insurance policy that will pay $1.5 million at her death. She wants to be sure her estate will not be liable for estate tax, so she wants to transfer ownership of her policy. However, there's no one Judith trusts enough to take the policy outright. With the controls she can impose through a trust, however, she decides it's safe to allow her sister, the person she's closest to, to be the trustee of a life insurance trust for the policy. She creates a formal trust and transfers ownership of the life insurance policy to that trust. After Judith's death, her sister will handle the money for the children under the terms of the trust document.

There are strict requirements governing life insurance trusts. For example:
- The life insurance trust must be irrevocable. If you retain the right to revoke the trust, you will be considered the owner of the policy, and the proceeds will be taxed as part of your estate when you die.
- You cannot be the trustee.
- You must establish the trust at least three years before your death. If the trust has not existed for at least three years when you die, the trust is disregarded for estate tax purposes, and the proceeds are included in your taxable estate.

Charitable Remainder Trusts

With a charitable remainder trust, you make an irrevocable gift of property to a tax-exempt charity while you are alive. You are entitled to receive a preestablished income from the property during your life, and you can achieve significant tax savings on both income and eventual estate tax. When you die, of course, the gift property must go to the charity.

For the wealthy, a charitable remainder trust can be a good way to make a donation and achieve some financial benefits. But if you don't want the property to go to a charity when you die, don't consider this kind of trust. The tax breaks will never equal the full worth of the gift property and the income you can earn from it.

For folks of more modest means, you can receive similar benefits, albeit of lesser dollar value, by making a gift to a "pooled" charitable trust, where your gift is combined with those of others.

> **EXAMPLE:** Josie donates $50,000 to a pooled income charitable trust. The charity takes Josie's gift and combines it with other funds in the pool. Josie gets the following benefits:
> - income for life (paid semiannually) based on a set percentage of the charitable trust's net earnings
> - an income tax deduction of $50,000, less the present value of her right to receive the income for the trust for her life (this value is determined according to complicated IRS actuarial tables), and
> - a $50,000 reduction in her taxable estate at death.

Generation-Skipping Trusts

If you're downright rich, you might want to consider establishing a "generation-skipping" trust for the benefit of your grandchildren. This is a trust that pays only income to the middle generation—your children. When the children die, the trust principal is divided among the final beneficiaries, your grandchildren. (You can create this type of three-generation trust when the beneficiaries are other relations, or even nonrelations, but in reality these trusts are almost always used for direct family generations.)

Special tax rules govern generation-skipping trusts. The property in the trust is included in your estate when you die. But the trust property, up to the value of the estate tax exemption for the year you die, is not included in the estates of any of the middle beneficiaries (the life beneficiaries). That means no additional tax is due when the children die and the grandchildren get the money.

The amount that can be passed under a generation-skipping trust is limited to the amount of the personal estate tax exemption for the year of death. This value is determined when you, the person who establishes the trust, die. Even if the trust property becomes worth $20 million, when the middle generation dies, no tax is due then.

If you leave property worth more than the estate tax exemption in a generation-skipping trust, it is subject to a stiff tax. Congress imposed the limit on these trusts to eliminate one of the estate tax dodges of the very rich. Before this limit, a multimillionaire, or billionaire, could leave vast sums of money in generation-skipping trusts, effectively eliminating estate tax in every other generation.

Obviously, establishing this sort of trust makes sense only if your children have enough money to get along with only the interest, not the principal, of the trust property. My very limited experience hearing about the actual plans of rich people indicates you'll likely be at least in double-digit millions before you'll need to consider a generation-skipping trust.

Disclaiming Gifts

Disclaimers can also be used to lower overall estate tax. A disclaimer is a beneficiary's right to decline a gift or inheritance. With a well-prepared estate plan, a declined gift goes to the next in line for that property, normally the alternate beneficiary.

Though a beneficiary has an independent right to disclaim a gift, this right is often expressly stated in a will or living trust, so the beneficiary clearly knows the disclaimer is okay with the person who left the property. Disclaimers are most frequently used to make a family's overall estate tax situation better.

> EXAMPLE: Marie-Françoise, in her late 70s and quite well off, inherits $700,000 from her brother Martin's estate. The alternate beneficiary is Marie-Françoise's granddaughter Lola, an aspiring singer of classic French cabaret songs. Marie-Françoise doesn't need the money, and if she accepts the gift, it will increase the size of her taxable estate. Martin's will expressly authorizes any beneficiary to disclaim a gift. Lola, whom Marie-Françoise loves, surely could use help. So, without worrying that she's not doing as Martin wanted, Marie-Françoise disclaims the gift, and it goes to Lola. ●

Property Control Trusts

Y ou may want to, or believe you need to, control how your property is managed and distributed for an extended period of time after your death. For instance, if you're in a second or subsequent marriage, you may want to ensure that your property ultimately goes to your children from a former marriage, while also allowing your current spouse some benefits from your property. Or you may want to leave property to someone who, for one reason or another, can't manage it for her- or himself, such as a child with a disability.

The usual way to impose controls over your property after your death is by creating a trust. Here we'll look at how you can use different types of what I call "property control trusts" to achieve your goals. (A related concern, leaving property to a minor or young adult, is discussed in Chapter 3.)

> ### SEE AN EXPERT
> **Most property control trusts are not a do-it-yourself job.** Except for the special needs trust discussed below, you'll need to hire an attorney if you want to create any of the trusts discussed in this chapter.

Marital Property Control Trusts for Second or Subsequent Marriages

In many second or subsequent marriages, one or both spouses may feel conflicted about estate planning. On one hand, a surviving spouse may well need use of or income from the deceased spouse's property, or may even need to spend some of that property to live comfortably. On the other hand, children from a former marriage may expect a large portion of that property soon after their parent dies.

Even if children aren't insistent, a parent may want to help with their financial needs. Further, even if children are willing to wait for their inheritance until both spouses die, the children may still be understandably concerned that their inheritance be preserved, not consumed by a surviving spouse. These kinds of problems—which can be dicey at the best of times—become even more complicated if your spouse and children from a former marriage don't get along well.

You may be able to use a distinctive type of trust, which I call a "marital property control trust," to reconcile your desires for your spouse and children. With this kind of trust, you name your spouse as the life beneficiary for trust property. (A life beneficiary has defined rights to use trust property during his or her life, but no right to leave that property to anyone.) You name your children or other inheritors as the final beneficiaries, to receive all trust property after your spouse dies. If your spouse doesn't survive you, the trust property goes directly to your final beneficiaries when you die. The life beneficiary of a marital property control trust usually has narrowly defined, restricted rights to the trust property.

Unmarried Couples

This chapter talks in terms of subsequent marriages and surviving spouses because most people who do this type of estate planning are married. But the principles apply equally to unmarried couples with children from previous relationships.

EXAMPLE: Tim and Margaurite are married; both are in their 50s. Tim has a son from his first marriage. Margaurite has two daughters from hers. The couple purchases a house for $1.6 million. Each contributes $200,000 toward the down payment; mortgage payments are shared equally. Each owns one-half of the house. When one spouse dies, each wants the other spouse to be able to live in the house for the remainder of his or her life. But after both have died, each wants his or her share of the house to go to the children of their first marriages. So Tim and Margaurite each create a marital property control trust. Each spouse's trust allows the surviving spouse full use of the house, but not the right to sell it. When the surviving spouse dies, half of the house goes to Tim's son, and the other half to Margaurite's two daughters.

The key to a marital property control trust is that the rights of the surviving spouse to trust property are specifically limited and controlled as defined in the other spouse's trust document. For instance, you may give your spouse the right to receive income from the trust property but no right whatsoever to spend trust principal. Or you can name someone else, not the surviving spouse, to be the trustee of the trust. This obviously reduces the surviving spouse's control over trust assets.

By placing sensible restrictions on your spouse's rights to trust property, you can feel confident that most or all of the trust principal will remain intact for your children. Marital property control trusts are, of course, no guarantee that family conflicts and tensions will be eliminated or even reduced. But they can provide legal control over your assets and give you the comfort that you've done your best to provide for both your spouse and your children.

Figuring out exactly what restrictions you want to impose on the trust property can become complicated fast. Before finalizing a marital property control trust, you may need to work through many complexities. Here's where an experienced and empathetic lawyer can help, by raising the right questions—but not by dictating your answers. For example, to return to the house in Tim and Margaurite's trust:

- Who should be the trustee? The surviving spouse? Or is it better to have a child share that job with the surviving spouse? Or to have a child be the sole trustee?
- Can the surviving spouse rent the house to someone else? If so, for any reason, or only if he or she cannot continue to occupy it for health reasons? What happens if the spouse no longer wants to live in the home? How long can the spouse leave the house vacant?
- If the house is rented, who decides what happens to the rental income? Can the surviving spouse use it to pay for his or her health needs? For any basic needs?

- How will you ensure that the house is properly maintained and all taxes and bills are paid?
- What reports and accountings of the trust property must the trustee give to the children?

Turning the answers to such questions into a binding, coherent legal document requires careful drafting—which is the major reason it will cost you a significant lawyer's fee to have a marital property control trust prepared.

Choosing the right trustee for a marital property control trust is vital. The trustee will have authority to manage the trust property and make any authorized payments to the surviving spouse. Also, the trustee may have the responsibility of making sure that the surviving spouse is using the trust property as dictated by the trust. These duties can require diplomacy or tough decision making.

> **EXAMPLE:** Leticia, in her 70s, marries Ben, in his 60s. Leticia has been married twice before and has one grown child from each marriage, a daughter, Lindsay, and a son, Kevin. Her estate consists of her house, worth $850,000 (all equity), plus savings and securities totaling $950,000. Ben owns much less, about $40,000 in savings. He also receives a modest pension plus Social Security.
>
> Ultimately, Leticia wants her property to pass equally to her two children. But if she dies before Ben, she doesn't want him thrown out on the street. She places her house and savings in a marital property control trust, giving Ben the right to live in the house and receive all income from the trust property during his life.
>
> Kevin has made it clear he does not care for Ben. Lindsay and Ben have a tolerable relationship, though they aren't close. Ben tells Leticia that he wants to be trustee, because he'd prefer not to have his well-being ruled by one of her children. Kevin tells Leticia that he's sorry to say it, but he thinks Ben is improvident and could squander her estate. Leticia doubts this, but

she doesn't want to take the risk. Kevin says he'd like to be the trustee. Although Kevin is a competent businessman, Leticia does not want to impose him on Ben. Lindsay, who's also levelheaded, tells Leticia she'd prefer not to be the trustee. But after considerable pondering, Leticia concludes that she has no one else she wants for the job. She persuades Lindsay that it will be best for all of them if she accepts the role of trustee, which she does. Then Leticia faces the delicate task of explaining her decision to Ben and Kevin, and trying to soothe any ruffled feelings.

The trust document gives Ben the right to remain in the house, with all its current furnishings, for his life. If he leaves it for more than four consecutive months, whether to move to some tropical paradise or a nursing home, the house and furnishings can be sold or rented if the trustee decides that's desirable. The trustee can either save that trust income as part of the trust principal, or spend it on Ben's needs.

Thus, Leticia leaves it up to Lindsay to decide what should happen to the house if Ben vacates it for more than four months. Leticia doesn't want to require that the house be turned over to her children in these circumstances. She just wants to protect her children, and not have the house stand empty for a long time. Leticia trusts Lindsay to make a wise decision if this matter comes up.

To stress the most vital point again, each marital property control trust involves the unique circumstances of the couple and final beneficiaries involved. There are no set rules dictating what's right. With this type of trust, you are inherently dealing with possible conflicts—the basic concern, after all, is that the surviving spouse's desires and interests may be very different from, or directly in conflict with, the desires and interests of the deceased spouse's children. Although you need a lawyer to help you work through issues about the trust, and draft the final version in clear language, the most important issues are practical, human ones: You must work out what's fair (as best you can) and decide who is best able to serve as successor trustee, overseeing your trust and carrying out your decisions. These concerns may be easy to state but, in real life, they can be quite difficult to resolve.

Special Needs Trusts for People With Disabilities

Parents or others who care about someone who has a serious disability can face difficult estate planning questions. Understandably, they want to provide for the loved one to whatever extent they can, for as long as that person lives.

However, planning for that loved one's financial future can be complicated because any gifts of property or money left directly to a person with a disability can result in ineligibility for essential government benefits. This leaves many folks who care for people with disabilities in a quandary—how can I help support my loved one without causing them to lose vital benefits?

One option is to make a special needs trust. Property left to a person in a special needs trust can be used to enrich that person's life, without jeopardizing government benefits. The trick is that the person with the disability never owns the property—the trust owns the property—so the property is not counted when the government assesses eligibility for benefits. Money or property in the trust is controlled and distributed to the beneficiary by the trustee of the trust.

Special rules apply to special needs trusts. Under U.S. Social Security Administration (SSA) guidelines, the property in a special needs trust doesn't affect eligibility for Social Security assistance if the beneficiary cannot:

- control the amount or frequency of trust payments, or
- revoke the trust and use the property.

In other words, the beneficiary must have no rights to demand and receive money from the trust income or principal. Nor can the beneficiary simply terminate the trust and take all the money in it. All control over payment of income or principal to the beneficiary must reside solely with the trustee. Normally, the trust gives the trustee the power to spend money on behalf of the beneficiary for carefully defined needs that are not met by government aid.

A primary concern with a special needs trust is making sure you select a trustee and one or more successor trustees who are willing and able to do the job. The trustee must be attentive to the beneficiary's situation, discerning what is needed and providing for those needs to the fullest possible extent. The trustee must stay in close contact with the beneficiary, so it is essential that the two get along. And finally, the trustee should have the savvy to deal with various institutions, from hospitals to banks to government agencies.

If there is no good choice for trustee, or if using a special needs trust seems too complicated, another option is to join a pooled special needs trust. Pooled trusts are "group" trusts in which families pool their money together for their loved ones. Pooled trusts are generally run by nonprofits that administer the trust and provide trustees. For families that don't have enough money to make a special needs trust worthwhile, pooled trusts offer an efficient and sensible solution.

RESOURCE

Learn more about special needs trusts. *Special Needs Trusts: Protect Your Child's Financial Future,* by Kevin Urbatsch and Michele Fuller-Urbatsch (Nolo), explains how special needs trusts work and provides all of the forms and instructions you need to make a special needs trust for a person with a disability. The book includes a detailed chapter on pooled trusts.

Education Trusts

If you want to create a structure to help pay for someone's college or other schooling, you can use an "education trust." These trusts are rarely set up by children's parents, who usually pay education costs directly. Commonly, grandparents or other older relatives create education trusts to aid young relations.

Creating an educational property control trust often involves complex issues including:

Deciding when the trust should become operational. If you are unlikely to live until a child begins college, you can arrange to have the trust begin at your death. But if the child is older, near or at college age, you may want the trust to become operational right away. Before setting up a trust that begins during your life, you need to look into the gift tax consequences. The property you give to the trust will be a taxable gift. The gift tax exemption for educational costs won't apply, because that works only for money paid directly to an educational institution. (See "Gifts for Medical Bills or School Tuition," in Chapter 9.)

Deciding how each beneficiary qualifies for benefits. People take many different approaches to education, and you'll need to think about what limits, if any, you want to place on your trust beneficiary or beneficiaries. For example, must a beneficiary reach a certain education level—such as college or graduate school—to receive payments from the trust? If so, what qualifies as a college or graduate school? Your grandchild may discover another way to learn—for example, working with a well-known chef or dancer. Would the trustee have authority to approve the payment for this?

If you name multiple beneficiaries, deciding whether the trustee can pay unequal amounts for them. Your beneficiaries are likely to have different financial needs, depending on the educational paths they follow. For instance, if one child goes to a very expensive college and then a more expensive graduate school, his or her education may require a large portion of the total trust assets. Would your trustee be authorized to pay the tuition bills in full? Suppose some beneficiaries are much younger than others. Must the trustee retain a certain percentage of trust assets for each beneficiary?

Deciding what happens if new (potential) beneficiaries are born. If you're creating a trust for a group, such as all your grandchildren, do you want the trustee to be able to make payments to new members of the group (new grandchildren) born after your death?

Deciding when the trust ends. You'll need to consider what should happen to any money left in the trust when no more beneficiaries are eligible for education payments. You might, for example, provide that all remaining money be divided equally among the beneficiaries. At another extreme, you could have the trustee decide how to distribute the money among the beneficiaries.

Facing these issues, you may wonder whether it's worth the effort to establish an education trust. Good question. Happily, though, for quite a number of older, wealthier individuals, an education trust does make sense. With a good lawyer, you can create exactly the trust you want without great difficulty. Whatever work this involves will most likely be far outweighed by the satisfaction of knowing that you have secured the educational future (or, at least the costs of that future) for people you love.

Spendthrift Trusts

If you want to leave property to an adult who just can't handle money sensibly, a "spendthrift trust" is a good idea. The purpose of this type of trust is to restrict the beneficiary's ability to squander trust money. The beneficiary has no direct ownership rights over the trust property and no right to pledge trust principal, or future income expected from the trust, as security for a loan. Thus, the beneficiary's creditors cannot seize the trust property if he or she gets into financial hot water.

With a spendthrift trust, the trustee is always a different person than the beneficiary. When you design the trust, you give the trustee power to spend trust money to fit your specific situation and desires. Perhaps you want to allow your trustee to spend any amount he or she wants for the beneficiary's needs. Or, you might limit the trustee to paying only housing costs for the beneficiary. On the other hand, you may want the trustee to make payments directly to the beneficiary, if the trustee decides that's wise. Of course, once the trustee has turned money over to the beneficiary, the controls of the trust are gone for that money.

At the extreme, a spendthrift trust can give the trustee power to cut off all payments, temporarily or even permanently, to a beneficiary who becomes uncontrollably self-destructive. Income withheld may be accumulated in the trust or paid to another beneficiary named in the trust document.

As with the other property control trusts discussed in this chapter, if you want to set up a spendthrift trust, get thee to a good estate planning lawyer.

Flexible Trusts

You may not want to decide now precisely how your property should be distributed when you die. Instead, you may want to leave this decision in the hands of someone you trust. You can accomplish this by creating a "sprinkling trust," authorizing your trustee to spend trust money among, or for, several beneficiaries you've named. A sprinkling trust can work well if you have both complete confidence in your trustee and a number of beneficiaries who may need varied payments over a long period of time.

The obvious difference between a sprinkling trust and all other property control trusts is that with the former you don't specify what property each beneficiary gets, or when. Rather, you leave money in a pot for two or more beneficiaries. (Indeed, a family pot trust for minors is one type of sprinkling trust. See "Trusts for Children," in Chapter 3.) The trustee alone decides which beneficiaries get payments, when, and how much. You can specify when the trust should end, and what happens to any money left in the trust, or you can leave these matters to the trustee. You may also impose certain limits on the trustee's discretion over trust property, such as requiring that each beneficiary receive at least 5% of trust income each year. ●

Lawyers

Must you hire an attorney to do your estate planning competently? You surely know my answer by now. As I've stated often in this book, with good self-help materials, many people can handle all their own estate planning work. Others will decide that they do need an attorney, for one or more sensible reasons. Then the concern becomes finding a good lawyer, for a fair fee.

Will You Need a Lawyer?

Every estate plan involves some legal documents—at least a will, usually a living trust, health care directive, durable power of attorney for finances, and perhaps other papers. Ask yourself whether you're willing and able to do some or all of the legal work for your estate planning. If you answer no, then you'll need to hire a lawyer. (Of course there's nothing wrong with this approach; it's your money and your time, and it's certainly not my job to tell you how to apportion the two.)

On the other hand, if you are willing to do your own legal work, and you have a relatively simple estate plan, you should be able to prepare the documents you want without hiring a lawyer. The key is that phrase "relatively simple." Roughly, it means having a straightforward beneficiary plan and an estate that won't be liable for estate tax.

You may, understandably, remain doubtful about preparing your own documents. Perhaps you feel that you can understand the basic concepts but are dubious about actually preparing the papers. Indeed, many people are so intimidated by estate planning that they fear that without a lawyer they'll do something wrong, and that their property won't be distributed as they wish.

The fact that so many people worry that estate planning requires a lawyer surely shows how fear-ridden our legal system has become. To dispel some of this fear, let's look realistically at what's involved when you prepare a will or living trust. The core transaction is generally quite simple: People just want to leave their property to whom they want to get it after they die. What's inherently complicated about that? Nothing. Indeed, as I've already noted, many people can state in a sentence or two what they want.

> **EXAMPLE 1:** I want all my property to go to my wife, Yvonne Kamner, or if she dies before I do, to be divided equally among my three children.

> **EXAMPLE 2:** I want my house and all my other property to go to my sister Charlotte O'Malley. If she dies before me, I want my property sold and the money divided equally among the Red Cross, the Audubon Society, and CARE.

> **EXAMPLE 3:** I want half the value of my property to go my husband, Bill Tarver, and the other half divided equally between my children, Christopher Reilly and Mona Reilly Jamison.

Do not believe the lawyers or estate planning books that tell you it's crazy to do your estate planning yourself. Preparing a basic will, living trust, medical directive, or financial durable power of attorney is not like creating a new computer or designing a house. Although very wealthy people may benefit from the services of a lawyer, if you're not looking for complicated estate planning maneuvers, you may well be able to safely prepare your own documents.

Let me stress one final point about deciding whether you need a lawyer. Your estate plan should express your intentions—and no one else can decide for you what those intentions are. Sometimes when people think, or fear, that they need a lawyer, what they are really doing is longing for an authority figure (or believing one is required) to tell them what to do. But only you can decide who should get your property, and how and when they should get it. If you want to talk things over with someone you trust, that's fine and good. However, at most, an estate planning expert should be your legal technician and adviser, not your mentor.

Working With a Lawyer

Lawyers are costly. There's a shock. Estate planning fees usually range from $200 to $500 per hour or more. But if your situation is complex and you want professional help, a good lawyer can be well worth the cost. Here's some thoughts on finding a lawyer you'll like.

Hiring a Lawyer to Review Your Estate Planning Documents

Hiring a lawyer solely to review the legal documents you create yourself may sound like a good idea. It shouldn't cost much, and it seems to offer a comforting security. Sadly, though, it may be difficult or even impossible to find a lawyer who will accept the job.

Though this is unfortunate, I'm not willing to excoriate lawyers who won't review do-it-yourself estate planning documents. From their point of view, they are being asked to accept what might turn into a significant responsibility for what they regard as inadequate compensation, given their usual fees. Any prudent lawyer sees every client as a potential occasion for a malpractice claim, or at least, serious later hassles—for example, a phone call four years down the line that begins, "I talked to you about my living trust, and now…." Most experienced lawyers want to avoid this kind of risk. Also, many lawyers feel that if they're only reviewing someone else's work, they simply don't get deeply enough into a situation to be sure of their opinions. Then there's the truth that beyond the few formal, legal requirements and technical exceptions, there's no one right way to prepare, say, a will or a living trust. Unfortunately, some lawyers think this means that if you haven't prepared your documents their way, you've done it wrong.

If you feel that you really need an attorney to review your documents, all I can suggest is that you keep trying to find a sympathetic lawyer—perseverance may pay off. Also be prepared to pay enough to make the lawyer feel adequately compensated for the work and assumption of responsibility.

Finding a Lawyer

If you want to hire a lawyer but don't know one, how do you find a lawyer who is trustworthy, competent, and charges fairly? A few words of advice may be helpful.

What Type of Lawyer Do You Need?

First, decide what type of lawyer you need. Estate planning lawyers fall into three categories:
- general practice lawyers
- estate planning specialists, and
- highly specialized lawyers working in one very difficult aspect of estate planning.

Which type is right for you depends on your estate planning concerns and needs.

- **General practice lawyers.** General practice lawyers handle all sorts of cases; they don't specialize in estate planning. If your needs are basic, such as a garden-variety living trust or will, or researching some aspect of your state's laws, a competent attorney in general practice should be able to do a good job at a lower cost than more specialized attorneys.
- **Estate planning specialists.** For any type of sophisticated estate planning work, ranging from estate-tax savings to property control trusts, you need to see a specialist. To do a good job with higher-end estate planning, a lawyer needs to be absolutely up to date on estate tax law and regulations, the rules governing ongoing trusts, and numerous other matters. Most general practice lawyers are simply not sufficiently educated in this field. An expert may charge relatively high fees, but a good expert is well worth it. Also, it's worth noting that if you need estate tax planning, you (or you and your spouse together) can surely afford it.

- **Highly specialized lawyers.** Some lawyers specialize in a particularly difficult aspect of estate law, such as multinational estate planning or preparing QDOT trusts for property left to noncitizen spouses. Another example is the preparation of complicated "special needs" trusts. To do a good job here, a lawyer must be current on complex federal and state regulations regarding trust property and eligibility for government benefits. Even most estate planning experts don't have sufficient expertise for this.

How to Look for a Lawyer

After you decide what type of lawyer you need, it's time to look for the individual who can best help you. You should actually enjoy working with your estate planning lawyer. Ideally, you'll find one with whom you have personal rapport and who treats you as an equal. From a lawyer's point of view (at least this lawyer), one of the best things about estate planning work is that you are not seeing people in crisis, and not making money off their misery, as so much lawyering does (accident victims, divorces, accused criminals, anyone in litigation). With good estate planning, everybody wins, except probate lawyers and the taxman.

When looking for a good lawyer, especially an estate planning expert, personal routes are the traditional, and probably best, method. If a relative or friend who has good business and financial sense knows an estate planning lawyer he or she recommends, chances are you'll like the lawyer too. Failing this, check with people you know in any political or social organization with which you're involved, especially those with a large number of members over age 40. Assuming they themselves are savvy, they may well be able to point you to a competent lawyer who handles estate planning matters and whose attitudes are similar to yours.

Another good approach is to ask for help from a lawyer you know personally and think well of, no matter what area that lawyer works in. Very likely the lawyer can refer you to someone trustworthy who is an estate planning expert.

RESOURCE

Finding a lawyer online. If you find yourself searching for a lawyer online, try these excellent (and free) resources that can help you eliminate some of the guesswork:

- **Nolo's Lawyer Directory.** Nolo has an easy-to-use online directory of lawyers, organized by location and area of expertise. You can find the directory and its comprehensive profiles at www.nolo.com/lawyers.
- **Lawyers.com.** At Lawyers.com you'll find a user-friendly search tool that allows you to tailor results by area of law and geography. You can also search for attorneys by name. Attorney profiles prominently display contact information, list topics of expertise, and show ratings—by both clients and other legal professionals.
- **Martindale.com.** Martindale.com offers an advanced search option that allows you to sort not only by practice area and location, but also by criteria like law school. Whether you look for lawyers by name or expertise, you'll find listings with detailed background information, peer and client ratings, and even profile visibility.

Yet another possibility is to check with people you respect who own their own small businesses. Almost anyone running a small business has a relationship with a lawyer, and chances are they've found one they like. Again, this lawyer will probably not be an estate planning expert, but he or she will likely know one, or several.

If you need a lawyer with highly specialized skills, such a person may be difficult to find. In some states, such as California, state bar associations certify lawyers as expert estate planners, but even this is no guarantee they are competent in one of the very specialized areas of estate planning. You simply have to seek until you find a lawyer you trust who has the expertise you need.

And finally, a warning: Be prudent with lawyer-referral services, often run by county bar associations, which will give you the names of some attorneys who practice in your geographic area. The referral service may provide only minimal screening for the attorneys listed, which means that those who participate may not be the most experienced or competent. It may be possible to find a skilled attorney willing to work for a reasonable fee following this approach, but be sure to ask the attorney about his or her credentials and experience.

Personally evaluate any lawyer you've been referred to before you agree to have the lawyer handle your estate plan. Don't hesitate to question the lawyer, no matter how expert he or she is considered to be.

No matter how charming and sympathetic your lawyer, be sure you've settled your fee arrangement—in writing—at the start of your relationship. In addition to the amount charged per hour, also get an estimate of how many hours your lawyer expects to put in on your matter.

Doing Your Own Research

Instead of hiring a lawyer, you may decide to do your own legal research. Of course, legal research isn't for everyone. You need energy, patience, and the ability and desire to enter a new mental world. If you're intrepid, however, you'll probably save money on attorneys' fees, and, hopefully, feel satisfied that you've acquired at least some sense of mastery over an area of law.

The best book explaining how to do your own legal work is *Legal Research: How to Find & Understand the Law,* by the Editors of Nolo (Nolo). It shows you, step by step, how to find answers in the law library, and it is, as far as I know, the only legal research book written specifically for nonprofessionals.

CAUTION
Don't get in too deep. While I applaud people who tackle their own legal research, I'll admit I've rarely found legal research to be much fun. And if you're investigating complicated legal issues, it can trip you up. You must be especially careful when investigating estate tax matters. The Internal Revenue Code is abstruse, dense, and potentially treacherous. If you want an estate tax-saving trust that may save your inheritors tens or hundreds of thousands of dollars, it's far wiser to hire an expert than to try to become one yourself.

You can do a lot of research online. If you want information about current estate planning issues, such as a recent court decision or a new statute, you'll probably be able to find it somewhere online. Many public libraries now offer Internet access, if you're not connected at home or work.

The Nolo website offers extensive materials on estate planning for no cost. You can find us at www.nolo.com. ●

Finalizing Your Estate Plan

Once you've decided on your estate plan and finalized the documents you want, are you all done? Basically, yes—except (ah, the eternal "except")—except for storing your documents and making any subsequent changes you decide are necessary. Here's a commonsense approach to storing your documents, and some basic rules about when and how to make changes to your plans.

Storing Your Estate Planning Documents

Finishing your estate plan means that you have created some important documents: a health care directive, a durable power of attorney for finances, a will, probably a living trust, and possibly others, ranging from pay-on-death accounts to revised business-ownership papers. Obviously, you need to keep all these documents in a safe place, where you and your executor, successor trustee, and attorney-in-fact can readily find them. This should be easy to accomplish. Any secure place can be used for storage: a safe in your house or office, or a drawer in your home desk or file cabinet. Using a bank safe-deposit box is probably overcautious, and possibly burdensome. Your executor may not have access to the box after your death, and there's a chance the box will be sealed if your estate owes state estate tax. In any case, the major worry with estate planning documents isn't that they'll be stolen (they have no street value, after all) but that they'll be lost. Using a secure place in your home or office, one that your executor/successor trustee and attorney-in-fact know about, should solve this worry.

You can make and distribute as many copies of your documents as you want. You may choose to give copies to beneficiaries and other concerned people so they know the details of your estate plan. For example, some people give a copy of their living trust to each beneficiary. You may also want to give copies of your health care directives to your attorney-in-fact, primary care physician, and local hospital. And it's often desirable to give copies of a durable power of attorney for finances to your attorney-in-fact and any institutions he or she will be dealing with. Finally, you may need copies of your estate planning documents for other reasons, such as demonstrating to a financial institution that you do have a valid living trust.

While using copies of a signed legal document is often helpful, making duplicate originals is always a bad idea. A duplicate original is a document prepared with the same formality as the first original. For example, a duplicate original will would be signed and dated by the will maker and witnesses, whereas a copy of an original will would just be a photocopy of the signed document. Duplicate originals are a bad idea because each original, whether first or duplicate, is a separate, legally valid document. If you later decide to amend or revoke the document, you must do so with every duplicate original. At best, this will be a hassle. At worst, you risk creating conflicting documents if you fail to amend or revoke any duplicate original.

Revising Your Estate Plan

Unlike contemporary art trends or haute couture clothes, estate plans are not designed for frequent change. Indeed, many people never need to revise or amend their plan. However, major life events frequently call for estate planning changes. If any of the following events occur, you should review your plan:

You get married. In the great majority of states, if you don't update your will, your new spouse will have the right under state law to inherit a certain portion of your estate. (See Chapter 2.)

You have or adopt a child. The rule here is similar to that for marriage. (See Chapter 2.)

You get divorced. In some states, a divorce ends a former spouse's right to inherit under a will. In other states, it doesn't. Also, property left to a divorced spouse using devices other than a will may not be affected by a divorce. If you've made a durable power of attorney for finances and named your former spouse as attorney-in-fact, divorce may terminate his or her authority, depending on your state.

A beneficiary dies. You'll want to revise your plan to arrange for alternate disposition of the affected property.

You want to put someone else in charge of your plans. For various reasons, you may want to change the executor of your will, or the successor trustee of your living trust. Or you may want to name a different attorney-in-fact under your durable power of attorney for health care or finances. You may also want to change the personal or property guardian you have named for your minor children or, if you have established a children's trust or pot trust, the person you have named as trustee or custodian for a gift under the UTMA.

Your financial or property situation changes significantly. This includes the sale or gift of any property you've specifically left to a named beneficiary.

You move to a new state. Your will and living trust remain legal and valid if you move to a different state after establishing them. However, there are a couple of reasons to check out some of your new state's estate planning laws. First, the new state might require a different form for health care documents or have different rules about finalizing a durable power of attorney for finances. Your old documents will most likely be honored in the new state, but your attorney(s)-in-fact will have an easier time if all your documents are made under the laws of your new home.

Second, if you are married and move from a common law state to a community property state or vice versa, you should learn how the laws of your new state affect marital property ownership. (To learn which states are community property states, see the list in Chapter 2.)

If you do decide to change your estate plan, you must usually decide whether you need, or want, to create entirely new documents or simply modify your existing ones. Generally, the more significant the changes, the more desirable it is to prepare a brand-new document. Also, if you prepared your original document in a format that is easily modified, such as a word processing program, software, or an online program, it may actually be easier to prepare a new document than to amend your old one.

If you do create a new document, you must formally revoke your old one. For example, most wills state near the beginning "I revoke all previous wills I have made," just to be sure any earlier will has been invalidated. You should also physically destroy—tear up—your old document. If you can round up any copies of your old document, it's sensible to destroy them, too. But you don't need to get hung up over this. As long as it is clear that you revoked the original of your old document, a copy of that old document cannot be used to invalidate your new document.

If you want to amend an existing document, what to do depends on the type of document at hand. An existing will can be amended by a formal document called a "codicil," a sort of legal "P.S." to the will. It must be executed with the formalities of a will, including using two witnesses.

A living trust can be revised fairly easily by a typed amendment. You must sign and date the amendment and have it notarized.

Other estate planning devices can also be easily changed. For instance, you can amend or revoke a pay-on-death account at any time. You can change a beneficiary simply by deleting the old one and entering a new one on the appropriate form. Indeed, as long as you are competent, you can change any part of your plan, except (there it is again) for certain irrevocable tax-saving trusts, such as a life insurance trust or a charitable remainder trust. ●

Some Sample Estate Plans

ometimes it's helpful to take a step back and look at the big picture of estate planning. This appendix contains some sample estate plans for a variety of families. These fictional plans aren't designed to describe every detail or step involved in estate planning, but they should give you a good sense for how these families approach and tailor their estate plan to meet their unique needs.

Leslie and Martin: A Couple in Their Late 50s

Leslie and Martin are married and have three adult children, ages 31, 27, and 19. They live in Washington, a community property state. The couple's major assets, all community property, are: their house in Seattle, worth $900,000, almost all equity; various retirement accounts; a savings account with roughly $100,000; a modest stock portfolio. Their net worth is roughly $1.3 million.

Leslie's and Martin's Goals

The couple does not have to concern themselves with estate tax. Their combined estate will almost surely be under the amount exempt from federal estate tax. The couple wants the surviving spouse to inherit all property of the deceased spouse. After both spouses have died, the couple wants their property to be divided equally among their three children, with specified possible exceptions. The couple has loaned money to each of their oldest two children. Their youngest is currently in his second year of college. Having paid for the oldest two children's college, the couple feels that their estate should first pay for their youngest's college costs, in the unlikely event he is still in college when both die. The couple also wants to avoid probate. And finally, each wants to be sure that the other has full power to act for him or her in the event of incapacity.

Leslie's and Martin's Plan

The couple creates a living trust, the centerpiece of their plan. They transfer their house, the savings account, and the stock account into their trust. Each also names the trust as alternate beneficiary for her or his retirement account. (They've each already named the other spouse as the beneficiary.)

They name each of their children as the final beneficiaries of the trust, to receive one-third of the trust property after both spouses have died. However, a specific limitation to this equal division is imposed in the trust, providing that the amount left to each final beneficiary must be adjusted by the amount provided on a schedule attached to the trust document. On that schedule, the couple lists the amount of money to be deducted from each of the older two children's shares—the amount each child owes the couple. The schedule also provides that if the youngest child is attending college full time when both parents have died, he shall receive $25,000 a year until he finishes college and that this adjustment shall be made before division of the trust property into three shares.

If, as the couple hopes, each of the oldest two children repays at least some of the money loaned to them, the couple can simply amend the trust and prepare a new schedule listing the new amounts still owed to them. Likewise, if their son graduates from college while the couple (or at least one of them) remains alive, the provision for payment of his college costs will become meaningless.

Each spouse also prepares a simple will, to handle transfer of minor assets like a car, and personal bank accounts. Finally, each prepares health care documents and a financial durable power of attorney, so that the other spouse has complete power to act for a spouse who has become incapacitated.

Michelle: A Single Mother in Her 40s

Michelle has one child, Theodore, age 11. The father has not been involved in Theodore's life. Michelle's major assets are: a house, with a substantial mortgage and about $70,000 in equity; a (sorely depleted) 401(k) program, currently worth $45,000; savings of $23,000; some valuable jewelry her mother left her. Her estate is about $176,000.

Michelle's Goals

Michelle's primary goal is to do all she can to protect Theodore if she dies while he is a child. Most important is who would raise Theodore if Michelle cannot. Secondly, Michelle wants to leave all her assets to be used for Theodore, with special emphasis on paying for his college costs.

Michelle's Plan

Michelle decides for now she needs only a will, not a living trust as well. In her will she nominates her sister Melinda to be the personal guardian for Theodore if Michelle dies while he is a minor. The two sisters have, of course, discussed this, and Melinda is willing to be guardian, if need be. Michelle believes she'd be excellent. Michelle prepares a letter explaining in detail why Melinda would be the best personal guardian and that Theodore's father has been uninvolved.

In her will, Michelle leaves all her property to Theodore. Her will provides that if she dies while Theodore is under age 21, she leaves him her property under the Uniform Transfer to Minors Act (UTMA) of Maine (her state). She names Melinda as custodian for that UTMA gift.

When Theodore turns 21, Michelle intends to prepare a revised estate plan. Perhaps by then she will have sufficient property that a living trust will be desirable. Also at that time, she'll review whether she wants Theodore to inherit all her property outright when she dies, or if she prefers to establish a child's trust, so that he wouldn't receive that property outright until he becomes 30 or 35.

Lastly, Michelle prepares health care documents and a financial durable power of attorney, naming Melinda to act for her if she becomes incapacitated.

Randy and Lisa: A Prosperous Older Couple

Randy and Lisa have prospered, raised four children, now have several grandchildren. Residents of Illinois, a common law state, they co-own property worth roughly $10 million. This does not includes their two retirement plans, worth over $800,000.

Randy's and Lisa's Goals

Randy and Lisa want to be sure their property avoids both estate taxes and probate. Each wants to leave his or her half of their property for the use of the other. When both spouses die, they want their property to be divided equally among their four children. They decide that they do not want to concern themselves with who will receive such property if one of their children dies before they both do—if that highly unlikely tragedy occurs, they'll revisit their estate plan at that time.

Randy's and Lisa's Plan

Randy and Lisa are cautious and prudent about money. (That's a big reason they amassed the wealth they have.) They understand that, as of now, their estates are not big enough to be subject to estate taxes. But they are concerned that estate taxes might become an issue if Congress later lowers the exemption or repeals "portability." So they decide to create a disclaimer living trust. In the trust, each leaves his or her property to the other, with an express right to disclaim any or all of that gift—so that, if necessary to save on estate taxes, the surviving spouse will have the option to disclaim the deceased spouse's property. All disclaimed property would go into a life estate-trust benefiting the surviving spouse. This would create two separate estates worth around $5.5 million, well protected from estate tax even if

Congress lowers the personal exemption or repeals portability. However, if there's no estate tax reason to separate their estates when the first spouse dies, the surviving spouse can simply accept the deceased spouse's property. Each spouse names the other as the beneficiary for his or her retirement program, and they name their children as equal alternate beneficiaries. Money from the retirement programs will be transferred to the beneficiary or beneficiaries without going through probate.

Each spouse also prepares a simple will, leaving any property subject to that will (not much) to the other spouse, with the children as alternate beneficiaries. Each spouse also prepares health care documents and a financial durable power of attorney, so that the other spouse has complete power to act for a spouse who has become incapacitated. Each names their daughter Jill as alternate agent, to act if the other spouse cannot.

Gail and Nick: A Young Married Couple

Gail and Nick have two young children, ages two years and four months. They live in California, a community property state. Each spouse is employed and they own their house (heavily mortgaged) in joint tenancy. They also own two cars, the well-used furnishings of their home, personal possessions such as computers, and small retirement accounts. They co-own a savings account with $23,000; Mark has another account with $6,000 in his name, which he had before they were married.

Gail's and Nick's Goals

Their main concern is providing for their children's care, both personal and financial if both parents die while their children are minors. They live in the San Francisco Bay Area and would like to choose a guardian who lives nearby. But they can't come up with a choice that works. The other local parents they know seem nearly overwhelmed with their own parental responsibilities. Gail and Nick choose not to burden any of these friends by asking them to assume more responsibility. Then the two ask themselves where else they would want their children to be raised. Both of them came from San Diego and loved growing up there. Nick's parents still reside there. So Gail and Nick contemplate their San Diego friends, until they settle on one for the guardian and one for the alternate guardian. Happily, each of their choices fully accepts the (possible) responsibility.

Gail's and Nick's Plan

Gail and Nick each prepare a simple will, naming their choices for their children's personal guardian and property guardian. Each leaves his or her property to the other spouse. Each names their children as alternate beneficiaries. In their wills, they establish a child's trust for each child, and name the personal guardian as trustee of each trust.

Finally, each prepares health care documents and a financial durable power of attorney authorizing the other spouse to act in case of incapacity.

Richard: A Single Man

Richard is a bachelor and has no children. He owns a limited partnership interest worth $160,000, savings of $77,000, stock currently worth $46,000, a retirement account worth $69,000, various treasured household items, and a prized art collection. He doesn't know what he could sell the collection for, but guesses it would be over $200,000.

Richard's Goals

Richard is most concerned with who will get his property. He wants to leave some to his sister, some to her two children, and many items to many friends. He spends considerable time pondering who should get what, especially from his art collection. He makes and revises several lists before he's satisfied with his selection of beneficiaries and choice of property each will receive.

Richard also wants to avoid probate, and to make provisions for what happens if he becomes incapacitated.

Richard's Plan

Richard prepares a living trust. In that trust, he specifies the many beneficiaries he's chosen and precisely identifies the property he's left to each one. Richard then transfers the bulk of his property to the trust. His household items and art collection are transferred simply by listing them, in general terms, on a trust schedule. He must, however, do more work to transfer the limited partnership interest, savings account, and stock account into the trust. He writes the office of the General Partner of the limited partnership to learn how he can transfer that interest into his trust. He learns that he must send in a copy of the trust document, and complete a special transfer form the partnership provides. Similarly, he must send a copy of the trust and another form to his brokerage company to transfer that account to the trust. Finally he completes a bank form to transfer that account.

Richard names his sister as the beneficiary for 60% of his retirement program, and each of her daughters as a 20% beneficiary.

Finally, he prepares a basic will, health care documents, and a durable power of attorney for finances. His sister has health problems, so he does not want to name her to act for him if he becomes incapacitated. One or both of his sister's daughters would be acceptable to him, but both live far away. So he chooses his best friend, Tom, who's willing to accept the job.

Clemencia and Pierre: A Couple in Their Second Marriage

Clemencia and Pierre are in their 60s and have been married for 11 years. They live in New York, a common law state. Each was married before. Clemencia has a son, Pedro, and a daughter, Nina, from her first marriage; Pierre has a daughter, Simone, from his first marriage. The couple does not have a prenuptial agreement. They live in the house Clemencia retained from her first marriage. Eight years ago, they refinanced the house to make major improvements. Since then, Pierre has made all the mortgage payments.

Clemencia's other major assets are: a retirement program worth over $250,000; savings of $90,000; undeveloped real estate worth $75,000; two expensive cars (she likes cars) worth over $130,000.

Pierre's major assets are: whatever his interest is in the house; a condo he rents out, currently worth about $260,000; a 401(k) with $115,000; a stock account worth $61,000; $96,000 in savings.

Clemencia's and Pierre's Goals

Each wants their children or child from their prior marriage to eventually inherit his or her property. But each also wants the surviving spouse to continue to live comfortably, and receive income from the deceased spouse's property. The couple also wants to avoid probate.

Clemencia's and Pierre's Plan

The couple realizes that they want a living trust, and that they'll need to work with a lawyer to prepare the trust they need. They have some matters to resolve. First, how will it be determined what Pierre's interest in the house is? Since he's made mortgage payments for eight years, and will continue to make them, it's fair that he obtain some interest in the house. It'll take some work to determine a method for calculating his interest over time. Next, how will the trust work to achieve the couple's possibly conflicting goals? Suppose a spouse dies and the survivor wants to sell the house and move to a smaller place, or a nursing home. Can a trust document provide for this, while simultaneously preserving the other (deceased) spouse's interest in the value of the house? Because there are a number of issues that need to be resolved in order to address each spouse's goals, they seek the advice of an experienced estate planning attorney.

The couple also prepares basic wills, health care documents, and durable powers of attorney for finances. ●

Index

⚖ NOLO **Save 15%** *off your next order*

Register your Nolo purchase, and we'll send you a
coupon for 15% off your next Nolo.com order!

Nolo.com/customer-support/productregistration

On Nolo.com you'll also find:

Books & Software

Nolo publishes hundreds of great books and software programs for consumers and
business owners. Order a copy, or download an ebook version instantly, at Nolo.com.

Online Forms

You can quickly and easily make a will or living trust, form an LLC or corporation,
apply for a provisional patent, or make hundreds of other forms—online.

Free Legal Information

Thousands of articles answer common questions about everyday legal issues,
including wills, bankruptcy, small business formation, divorce, patents,
employment, and much more.

Plain-English Legal Dictionary

Stumped by jargon? Look it up in America's most up-to-date source for
definitions of legal terms, free at Nolo.com.

Lawyer Directory

Nolo's consumer-friendly lawyer directory provides in-depth profiles of lawyers all
over America. You'll find information you need to choose the right lawyer.

ESPN10